The move to global war
Study and Revision Guide

PAPER 1

Russell Quinlan

HODDER
EDUCATION

The Publishers would like to thank the following for permission to reproduce copyright material.

Photo credits: p11 Rykoff Collection/CORBIS/Corbis via Getty Images; **p22** Photograph © 2017 Museum of Fine Arts, Boston; **p28** State Historical Society of Missouri; **p33** British Cartoon Archive/Solo Syndication; **p46** Courtesy of the Jay N. 'Ding' Darling Wildlife Society; **p52** Poster of soldier, child, and doves, Poster Collection, CC 284, Hoover Institution Archives; **p59** Image courtesy of Roderick M. Barron - Barron Maps - www.barronmaps.com; **p78** British Cartoon Archive/Solo Syndication; **p81** © The Heartfield Community of Heirs/VG Bild-Kunst, Bonn and DACS, London 2017; **p89** IMAGNO/Austrian Archives (S)/TopFoto; **p100** British Cartoon Archive/Solo Syndication; **p106** Randall Bytwerk.

The publishers would like to thank the following for permission to reproduce material in this book: Penguin Books for extracts from *The Origins of the Second World War* by A.J.P. Taylor, published by Penguin Books, UK, 1991.

Acknowledgements: ABC-CLIO, *Events that Formed the Modern World* by Frank W. Thackery and John E. Findling, 2012. Allen Lane, *1939: Countdown to War* by Richard Overy, 2009. Association for Diplomatic Studies and Training, Excerpt of an interview given by Robert A. Fearey to the Association for Diplomatic Studies and Training in 1998. Avalon Project, Yale University, The Japanese Note to the United States United States, 1941; *The British War Bluebook*, 1934; *The French Yellow Book*, 1938; Franco-German Declaration of 6 December 1938; *Nazi Conspiracy and Aggression*, Volume 1, 1946. Blackwell Publishers, *The Causes of the Second World War* by Anthony Crozier, 1997. Cambridge University Press, *The Wars for Asia, 1911–1949* by S.C.M. Paine, 2012; *Mussolini Unleashed 1939–1941: Politics and Strategy in Fascist Italy's Last War* by MacGregor Knox, 1982; Cambridge University Press, *Social Darwinism in European and American Thought, 1860–1945: Nature as Model and Nature as Threat* by Mike Hawkins, 1997. Center for History and New Media, University of Missouri-Kansas City, *The Imperial Rescript on Education* by the Roy Rosenzweig Center for History and New Media. Columbia University Press, *Sources of Japanese Tradition*, compiled by William Theodore de Bary, Carol Gluck, and Arthur E. Tiedemann, 2006. Free Press, *The Age of Hirohito: In Search of Modern Japan* by Daikichi Irokawa, 1995. Greenwood Press, *The History of Poland* by M.B. Biskupski, 2000. Grove Press, *Hitler's Generals*, edited by Correlli Barnett, 1989. History Review, 'The Nazi Economy – Was It Geared to War?' by Richard Overy, 1998. Hogarth Press, *Why the German Republic Fell: And Other Studies of the Causes and Consequences of Economic Inequality*, edited by Arthur Madsen, 1941. Holmes & Meier, *The League of Nations: Its Life and Times, 1920–1946* by F.S. Northedge, 1986. Institute of Pacific Relations, *The Struggle for North China* by George E. Taylor, 1940. *Japan Times*, 1936 coup failed, but rebels killed Japan's 'Keynes' by Jeff Kingston, 2016. Library of Congress, Letter from US President Theodore Roosevelt to Senator Know, 1909, Papers of Theodore Roosevelt. Little Brown & Co., *The European World: A History*, second edition by Jerome Blum et al., 1970. Longman, Green & Co., *Japan Among the Great Powers: A Survey of Her International Relations* by Seiji Hishida, 1939. Macmillan, *Italian Fascism, 1919–1945* by Philip Morgan, 1995. Mainichi Newspapers, *Fifty Years of Light and Dark: The Hirohito Era* by the staff of the *Mainichi Daily News*, 1975. Modern Age Books, *You Might Like Socialism: A Way of Life for Modern Man* by Corliss Lamont, 1939. Nelson-Hall, *Haile Selassie I: Ethiopia's Lion of Judah* by Peter Schwab, 1979. Oxford University Press, *A Modern History of Japan: From Tokugawa Times to the Present* by Andrew Gordon, 2003; *Modern Japan: A History in Documents* by James L. Huffman, 2004. Pearson Education, *The Origins of the Second World War in Europe*, second edition by P.M.H. Bell, 1998; *The Inter-War Crisis: 1919–1939*, second edition by R.J. Overy, 2007; *The Origin of the Second World War in Europe*, second edition by P.M.H. Bell, 1998. Penguin Books, *The Road to War* by Richard Overy and Andrew Wheatcroft, 1999. Princeton University Press, *The Autobiography of Ozaki Yukio: The Struggle for Constitutional Government in Japan* by Ozaki Yukio, 2001. Public Affairs Press, *From the Marco Polo Bridge to Pearl Harbor: Japan's Entry into World War II* by David J. Lu, 1961. Routledge, *Emperor Hirohito and Shōwa Japan: A Political Biography* by Stephen S. Large, 1992; *The Manchurian Crisis and Japanese Society, 1931–33* by Sandra Wilson, 2002. Springer, *Sir Gerald Fitzmaurice and the World Crisis: A Legal Advisor in the Foreign Office 1930–1945* by Anthony Carty, 2000. University of British Columbia Press, *Japanese Diplomacy in a Dilemma: New Light on Japan's China Policy, 1924–1929* by Nobuya Bamba, 1972. University of Exeter Press, *Documents on Nazism 1919–1945* by Jeremy Noakes and Geoffrey Pridham, 1995. University of Tokyo Press, *Emperor Hirohito and His Chief Aide-de-Camp: The Honjō Diary, 1933–36* by Honjō Shigeru, translated by Mikiso Hane, 1982. US Government Printing Office, *Peace and War: United States Foreign Policy, 1931–1941* by the US Department of State, 1943; *Nazi Conspiracy and Aggression*, Volume I, compiled by the Office of the United States Chief of Counsel for Prosecution of Axis Criminality, 1946. W.W. Norton & Co., *Lend Me Your Ears: Great Speeches in History* by William Safire,, 2004. World Future Fund, 'The Doctrine of Fascism' by Benito Mussolini, 1932. *World Post*, 'Poland Caused WW II: Russian Report' by Mike Eckel, 2009.

Every effort has been made to trace all copyright holders, but if any have been inadvertently overlooked, the Publishers will be pleased to make the necessary arrangements at the first opportunity.

Although every effort has been made to ensure that website addresses are correct at time of going to press, Hodder Education cannot be held responsible for the content of any website mentioned in this book. It is sometimes possible to find a relocated web page by typing in the address of the home page for a website in the URL window of your browser.

Hachette UK's policy is to use papers that are natural, renewable and recyclable products and made from wood grown in well-managed forests and other controlled sources.
The logging and manufacturing processes are expected to conform to the environmental regulations of the country of origin.
Orders: please contact Hachette UK Distribution, Hely Hutchinson Centre, Milton Road, Didcot, Oxfordshire, OX11 7HH.
Telephone: +44 (0)1235 827827. Email education@hachette.co.uk Lines are open from 9 a.m. to 5 p.m., Monday to Friday.
You can also order through our website: www.hoddereducation.com.

ISBN: 978 1 5104 3234 5

© Russell Quinlan 2018

First published 2018 by
Hodder Education,
An Hachette UK Company
Carmelite House
50 Victoria Embankment
London EC4Y 0DZ

www.hoddereducation.com

Impression number   10 9 8 7 6 5 4 3 2
Year   2022 2021

Cover photo © Culture Club/Getty Images
Produced and typeset in Goudy and Frutiger by Gray Publishing, Tunbridge Wells
Printed in Spain

A catalogue record for this title is available from the British Library.

Contents

How to use this book

- Welcome to the *Access to History for the IB Diploma: The move to global war: Study and Revision Guide*. This book has been written and designed to help you develop the knowledge and skills necessary to succeed in the Paper 1 examination. The book is organized into double-page spreads.
- On the left-hand page you will find a summary of the key content you will need to learn. Words in bold in the key content are defined in the Glossary and Key figures list (see pages 108–11).
- On the right-hand page you will find exam-focused activities related to and testing the content on the left-hand side. These contain historical sources such as text excerpts or photos and cartoons and questions so that you can develop analytical and critical-thinking skills. Answers can be found at the back of the book.
- At the end of each chapter you will find an exam focus section. Here, you will find student answer examples with examiner comments and annotations to help you understand how to improve your grades and achieve top marks. There is also a 'mock exam' set of questions for you to try.

Together, these two strands of the book will provide you with the knowledge and skills essential for examination success. Student answer examples are provided, with commentary and examiner comments and annotations.

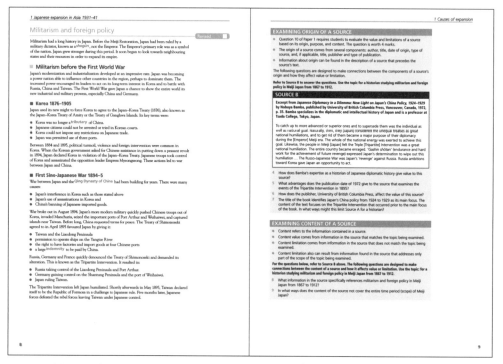

Key historical content   Exam-focused activities

At the end of the book, you will find:

- Glossary, Key figures and Timeline – key terms in the book are defined, key figures are highlighted and key dates are included in a timeline.
- Answers for the exam-focused activities.

Getting to know the exam

The four questions on Paper 1 assess different skills and knowledge. You must answer all four and have one hour to do so. For Paper 1, The move to global war, questions are numbered 9–12. The question types are as follows:

■ Question 9: direct questions

Question 9 is worth 5 marks and has two parts, both of which test your reading comprehension abilities on two different sources. You need to answer both parts of the question by reviewing the source material and paraphrasing information from the sources.

■ Question 10: value and limitations of a source

Question 10 is worth 4 marks and asks you to **evaluate** a source using the source's origin, purpose and the content you are presented with.

- The origin of a source is its author or creator. This might include the date, publisher and type of delivery, which could be a book, speech, propaganda poster or diary entry.
- The purpose of the source explains what the author was trying to do, such as explaining the impact of an event or conveying a certain type of information.
- The content of the source can indicate many things, such as the point of view of the author, evidence of some historical event or its interpretation or, in the case of a cartoon or other visual source, the audience that the creator wished to reach.

The values and limitations will vary according to each source. A value could be that the author of the source witnessed the event or is an acknowledged scholar. An example of a limitation could be that an author was involved in events and therefore may be less objective. You should try to explain at least two values and two limitations per source, although this may not always be possible.

■ Question 11: compare and contrast

Question 11 is worth 6 marks and asks you to **compare and contrast** two sources in terms of what information they convey to historians studying some aspect of this prescribed subject.

- Comparing means that you explain the similarities between the sources.
- Contrasting explains how they are different.
- You should aim to have about three similarities and three differences.

■ Question 12: essays integrating knowledge and sources

Question 12 is worth 9 marks and requires you to use all the sources in the examination, and to integrate them into an essay that also contains your own knowledge.

■ The appearance of the examination paper

■ Cover

The cover of the examination paper states the date of the examination and the length of time you have to complete it: one hour. Instructions are limited and simply state that you should not open it until told to do so and that all questions must be answered.

■ Sources

Once you are allowed to open your examination paper, you can turn to Prescribed subject 3: The move to global war. There you will see four sources, each labelled with a letter. There is no particular order to the sources, so Source A could potentially be a map, a speech, a photograph or an extract from a book. Source A is no more or less important than Source B, or Sources C or D. If you see square brackets, [ ], then this is an explanation or addition to the source by the creators of the examination and not part of the original source. Sometimes sources are shortened and you will see an ellipsis, three full stops (…), when this happens.

■ Questions

After the four sources, the four questions will appear. You need to answer all of them. It is better to answer the questions in order, as this will familiarize you with all the sources to be used in the final essay on question 12, but this is not required. Be sure to number your questions correctly. Do not use bullet points to answer questions, but instead write in full sentences when possible. Each question indicates how many marks it is worth, for example, [2].

Good luck with your studies and the exam!

Japanese expansion in Asia 1931–41

1 Causes of expansion

Revised

The impact of Japanese nationalism and militarism on foreign policy

Revised

The **Meiji Restoration** established the **Meiji Emperor** as the head of government in Japan, ending centuries of **feudalism**. The new government introduced a series of reforms, causing many tensions in Japan. Eventually, an **ultranationalist** state developed, with increasing power and influence of the military.

▥ The Meiji Constitution

The **Meiji Constitution** was given as a gift by the Emperor to the people of Japan in 1889. It made the Emperor of Japan head of state and declared him to be a divine individual. It also established a parliament, known as the **Diet**. Much political power, however, developed among members of the **Privy Council, cabinet** and military.

● The Emperor of Japan was head of state and a divine individual, giving him supreme authority.
● The Privy Council acted as advisors to the Emperor and controlled access to him.
● The cabinet consisted of ministers responsible for the various functions of government and reported to the Emperor.
● The military was granted a lot of independence in the constitution and was directly responsible to the Emperor. They used their positions in the cabinet to gain more power by threatening vetoes of laws that could cause the collapse of government.
● The Diet consisted of two bodies. The House of Representatives was elected by those with **suffrage**. They could create and pass laws. The House of Peers could approve or reject laws passed by the House of Representatives.

▥ Education and loyalty to the state

Education was mandatory for all citizens. After some opposition to government grew, the curriculum changed to emphasize loyalty and to value the Emperor, his divinity and Japan's uniqueness in the world and in history.

Changes to education helped in the growth of ultranationalism, also known as **radical nationalism**. This was similar to **fascism**. When military-type training was introduced to schools during the 1920s, the connection between education, the military and nationalism strengthened the appeal of the military throughout the country.

▥ The rise of radical nationalism

Japan's uniqueness was a key characteristic of ultranationalism and radical nationalism.

▰ Special mission

The Japanese believed they were on a special mission. What made Japan special?

● The Emperor was divine.
● It had never been conquered by Europeans or Americans.
● It had a long history of independence.
● Most citizens were Japanese who shared a common culture and history.
● It was the only non-European state to win a war against a European state through the Russo-Japanese War, 1904–5.
● It was a major power both militarily and industrially.

Japan's unique characteristics gave it a special mission to lead all of Asia and remove all non-Asian influences from the region.

Radical nationalism formed when the idea that anything that harmed Japan's Emperor and Japan must be prevented. Radical nationalists used threats and assassinations to protect Japan and achieve its special mission.

■ Growth of militarism

A strong military with a large navy and army was needed to achieve the special mission. The move towards militarism strengthened. The military held increasing power and influence in Japanese politics.

MIND MAP

Use the information from the opposite page to add details to the mind map below.

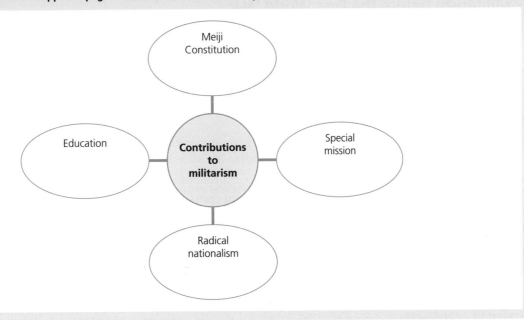

IDENTIFYING RELEVANT CONTENT

- For Paper 1, The move to global war, questions are numbered from 9 to 12.
- The first question of Paper 1 contains two parts (9a and 9b), both of which test reading understanding of two different sources. The two parts of question 9 should take about five minutes to answer.
- Question 9a is always a narrative excerpt.
- Students are asked to identify three main points from the source. This part of the question is worth 3 marks. That means three main points must be identified. Do not go into too much detail.
- **Note:** the phrase 'main points' means important understandings from the source. It **does not** mean simply listing facts from the source.

Read Source A and then answer the following questions that focus on identifying relevant content.

SOURCE A

Excerpt from *A Modern History of Japan: From Tokugawa Times to the Present* by Andrew Gordon, published by Oxford University Press, New York, USA, 2003, p. 92. Gordon is a professor of history at Harvard University and a former Director of the Reischauer Institute of Japanese Studies.

It is no surprise that the [Meiji Constitution] formally promulgated [to officially put into effect] in a grand ceremony in 1889 was written and presented in a way that sought to maximize the power of the state and minimize that of the people ... [It] was drafted secretly in 1886 and 1887 by a talented group under the direction of Itō Hirobumi and Inoue Kowashi. Itō studied European constitutions in Europe ... The document was discussed by top government officials in 1888 in a body newly created for this purpose, the Privy Council. This council continued to function as an extra-constitution advisory group once the constitution was promulgated. It served as a site where the Meiji leaders could manage the political system. This small group of leaders came to be known as Meiji 'oligarchs' (*genrō* in Japanese) ... The *genrō* were an informal body, in the sense that there was no constitutional provision for them ... [However] for the rest of their lives, they continued to pull the strings of politics, but as they grew older they stepped back from the front lines of political battle to positions such as the leadership of the Privy Council.

1 What were the main aims in terms of political power of the men who wrote the Meiji Constitution?
2 What function did the Privy Council play in Japanese politics?
3 What does it mean 'to pull the strings of politics' and how does this phrase show the influence of the Privy Council on political matters?

Militarism and foreign policy

Revised

Militarism had a long history in Japan. Before the Meiji Restoration, Japan had been ruled by a military dictator, known as a *shogūn*, not the Emperor. The Emperor's primary role was as a symbol of the nation. Japan grew stronger during this period. It soon began to look towards neighbouring states and their resources in order to expand its empire.

▧ Militarism before the First World War

Japan's modernization and industrialization developed at an impressive rate. Japan was becoming a power nation able to influence other countries in the region, perhaps to dominate them. The increased power encouraged its leaders to act on its long-term interest in Korea and to battle with Russia, China and Taiwan. The First World War gave Japan a chance to show the entire world, especially China and Germany, its new industrial and military prowess.

■ Korea 1876–1905

Japan used its new might to force Korea to agree to the Japan–Korea Treaty (1876), also known as the Japan–Korea Treaty of Amity or the Treaty of Ganghwa Island. Its key terms were:

- Korea was no longer a **tributary** of China.
- Japanese citizens could not be arrested or tried in Korean courts.
- Korea could not impose any restrictions on Japanese trade.
- Japan was permitted the use of three ports.

Between 1884 and 1895, political turmoil, violence and foreign intervention were common in Korea. When the Korean government asked for Chinese assistance in putting down a peasant revolt in 1894, Japan declared Korea in violation of the Japan–Korea Treaty. Japanese troops took control of Korea and assassinated the opposition leader, Empress Myeongseong. These actions led to war between Japan and China.

■ First Sino-Japanese War 1894–5

War between Japan and the **Qing Dynasty of China** had been building for years. There were many causes:

- Japan's interference in Korea such as those stated above
- Japan's use of assassinations in Korea
- China's banning of Japanese imported goods.

War broke out in August 1894. Japan's more modern military quickly pushed Chinese troops out of Korea, invaded Manchuria, seized the important ports of Port Arthur and Weihaiwei, and captured islands near Taiwan. Before long, China requested terms for peace. The Treaty of Shimonoseki, agreed to in April 1895, favoured Japan by giving it:

- Taiwan and the Liaodong Peninsula
- permission to operate ships on the Yangtze River
- the right to have factories and import goods at four Chinese ports
- a large **indemnity** to be paid by China.

Russia, Germany and France quickly denounced the Treaty of Shimonoseki and demanded its alteration. This is known as the Tripartite Intervention. It resulted in:

- Russia taking control of the Liaodong Peninsula and Port Arthur
- Germany gaining control of the Shantung Peninsula and the port of Weihaiwei
- Japan ruling Taiwan.

The Tripartite Intervention left Japan humiliated. Shortly afterwards in May 1895, Taiwan declared itself to be the Republic of Formosa in a challenge to Japanese rule. Five months later, Japanese forces defeated the rebel forces, leaving Taiwan under Japanese control.

EXAMINING ORIGIN OF A SOURCE

- Question 10 of Paper 1 requires students to evaluate the value and limitations of a source based on its origin, purpose and content. The question is worth 4 marks.
- The origin of a source comes from several components: author, title, date of origin, type of source, and, if applicable, title, publisher and type of publication.
- Information about origin can be found in the description of a source that precedes the source's text.

The following questions are designed to make connections between the components of a source's origin and how they affect value or limitation.

Refer to Source B to answer the questions. Use the topic: for a historian studying militarism and foreign policy in Meiji Japan from 1867 to 1912.

SOURCE B

Excerpt from *Japanese Diplomacy in a Dilemma: New Light on Japan's China Policy, 1924–1929* by Nobuya Bamba, published by University of British Columbia Press, Vancouver, Canada, 1972, p. 35. Bamba specializes in the diplomatic and intellectual history of Japan and is a professor at Tsuda College, Tokyo, Japan.

To catch up to more advanced or superior ones and to supersede them was the individual as well as national goal. Naturally, then, they [Japan] considered the unequal treaties as great national humiliations, and to get rid of them became a major purpose of their diplomacy during the [Emperor] Meiji era. The whole of the national energy was exerted to achieve this goal. Likewise, the people in Meiji [Japan] felt the Triple [Tripartite] Intervention was a great national humiliation. The entire country became enraged. '*Gashin shōtan*' (endurance and hard work for the achievement of future revenge) expressed Japan's determination to wipe out this humiliation … The Russo-Japanese War was Japan's 'revenge' against Russia. Russian ambitions toward Korea gave Japan an opportunity to act.

4   How does Bamba's expertise as a historian of Japanese diplomatic history give value to this source?

5   What advantages does the publication date of 1972 give to the source that examines the events of the Tripartite Intervention in 1895?

6   How does the publisher, University of British Columbia Press, affect the value of this source?

7   The title of the book identifies Japan's China policy from 1924 to 1929 as its main focus. The content of the text focuses on the Tripartite Intervention that occurred prior to the main focus of the book. In what ways might this limit Source A for a historian?

EXAMINING CONTENT OF A SOURCE

- Content refers to the information contained in a source.
- Content value comes from information in the source that matches the topic being examined.
- Content limitation comes from information in the source that does not match the topic being examined.
- Content limitation also can result from information found in the source that addresses only part of the scope of the topic being examined.

For the questions below, refer to Source B above. The following questions are designed to make connections between the content of a source and how it affects value or limitation. Use the topic: for a historian studying militarism and foreign policy in Meiji Japan from 1867 to 1912.

8   What information in the source specifically references militarism and foreign policy in Meiji Japan from 1867 to 1912?

9   In what ways does the content of the source not cover the entire time period (scope) of Meiji Japan?

■ Russia

Russia emerged as Japan's primary challenger. Tensions between the two countries centred on the Liaodong Peninsula and Port Arthur. Japan's economy benefited from its rapid industrialization. Rapid economic growth allowed Japan to enlarge its army and navy. Japan also began looking for allies.

■ Anglo-Japanese Alliance 1902

Russia also was rapidly industrialized and looked to expand into China. Concerned with Russian intent in China, Britain and Japan formed the Anglo-Japanese Alliance of 1902. The alliance reassured Japan that a war with Russia would not expand into a wider war with other countries as those countries would then be at war with Britain, a world power. Japan could now provoke a war against Russia with a greater confidence of victory.

■ Russo-Japanese War 1904–5

Tensions between Russia and Japan had continually increased since the Tripartite Intervention. Consequent Russian actions in China and Korea provoked Japan. Russia:

- leased Port Arthur and parts of the Liaodong Peninsula from China
- stationed warships in Port Arthur and fortified its defences
- began construction of a railway linking Port Arthur to Russia through Manchuria, a province of China
- pressured Korea for mining and forestry rights
- stationed a large army in Manchuria as protection from the **Boxer Rebellion** and kept it there after the rebellion failed.

Diplomatic talks between the two countries failed when a Japanese proposal to establish **spheres of influence** in the region was ignored by Russia. Japan expelled the Russian ambassador and ended all relations between the two countries. The war started soon afterwards.

- Japan attacked the Russian navy in Port Arthur in February 1904.
- Japan then invaded Korea and Manchuria.
- Port Arthur came under siege from the Japanese.
- In December 1904, Japanese artillery destroyed the Russian fleet in Port Arthur.
- The Japanese army won a major land battle at Mukden in Manchuria, taking control of that city in one of the largest battles of the twentieth century.
- The Japanese navy completely destroyed a Russian fleet at the Battle of Tsushima Straits.
- Japan occupied Sakhalin Island, claimed by Russia.
- The 1905 Revolution broke out in Russia, partially caused by Russian military defeats, forcing the Russian government to seek peace.

■ Treaty of Portsmouth 1905

The USA helped in negotiations of the Treaty of Portsmouth signed by Japan and Russia in September 1905. The terms of the treaty:

- required all troops to leave Manchuria and return it to Chinese control
- permitted Japan to lease the Liaodong Peninsula and Port Arthur from China
- granted Japan the right to lease the Southern Manchurian Railway, built by Russia, from China
- gave Japan the southern half of Sakhalin Island
- recognized Japan's claim on Korea.

Japan received additional international benefits from their victory in the Russo-Japanese War:

- international respect
- control of Korea in return for allowing the USA full control of the Philippines
- British recognition of Japan's right to control Korea
- an extension of the Anglo-Japanese Alliance.

At home, Japan's military enjoyed increased prestige as well as increased government spending for its programmes. But, Japan was not completely satisfied with the outcome of the war and the peace treaty. Japan felt it deserved:

- a war indemnity from Russia to pay for the war
- all of Sakhalin Island
- complete control of the Liaodong Peninsula, Port Arthur and parts of Manchuria instead of renting them from China.

IDENTIFYING RELEVANT CONTENT FROM AN ILLUSTRATION

- The first question of Paper 1 contains two parts (9a and 9b), both of which test reading understanding of two different sources. The two parts of question 9 should take about five minutes to answer.
- Question 9b is always a non-text source, usually an illustration, for example, a political cartoon, propaganda poster, photograph, and so on.
- Students are asked to identify two main messages or points from the source. This part of the question is worth 2 marks.
- Do not spend too much time on the response. List two messages from the source and no more. Two sentences are enough to fulfil the demands of this question.

Examine the following illustration and then answer the following questions that focus on identifying relevant content.

10 How does the size of the two figures in the postcard show Russian attitudes about the power of Russia compared to the power of Japan?

11 What does the text indicate about Russian beliefs about war with Japan?

12 In what ways does the illustration indicate racism?

SOURCE C

'Don't twist in my hands! I want to see how your skin tears on my teeth!' A Russian postcard from just before the Russo-Japanese War depicting a Russian Cossack (warrior) eating a Japanese soldier for breakfast, about 1904.

CONNECTING ORIGIN AND CONTENT TO VALUE AND LIMITATION

Use Source C to identify origin and content and connect them to value and limitation for a historian studying the Russo-Japanese War. Use the table to record your thoughts. In the first column, record key information about the source. In Value, connect the key information to how it is valuable to a historian. In Limitations, connect the key information to how it has limitations for a historian.

	Key information	Value	Limitations
Type of source			
Date created			
Perspective issues			
Purpose			
Content			

■ The First World War

The First World War provided an opportunity for Japan to show the world, especially Germany and China, that it was a great power.

■ Shantung Peninsula 1914

Britain asked Japan to enter the war as an ally in accordance with the Anglo-Japanese Alliance. Germany possessed a fortress in the harbour at Tsingtao on China's Shantung Peninsula, where it stationed warships. With Japan about to move on the Shantung Peninsula, Germany removed its warships. Tsingtao quickly surrendered to Japan. Japan also quickly took control of German possessions in the Pacific Ocean.

■ China 1915

With most of the attention of the war on Europe, Japan took advantage of China's weaknesses to assert its power. In January 1915, Japan issued the Twenty-One Demands to China. These demands would greatly increase Japan's power and presence in China, giving it a great degree of economic and political autonomy there, especially in Manchuria. Eventually the demands were reduced to thirteen. China agreed to these demands because it was not able to resist Japan. Anti-Japanese sentiment swept across China. The USA and Britain became concerned with Japanese aggression in China. These concerns influenced negotiations and decisions at the Paris Peace Conference.

■ Paris Peace Conference 1919

Japan was one of the victorious powers at the Paris Peace Conference. It was a founding member of the **League of Nations**. All League members accepted the idea of collective security, where war against one member was war against all members, and that members would seek to settle disputes diplomatically instead of militarily.

Japan and other non-European countries sought a clause against racial discrimination be included in the League of Nations' covenant. The USA refused to allow such a clause due to racial discrimination and segregation in the USA. Racial discrimination and segregation could be found in many European colonies as well. Therefore, the Europeans were also not interested in any such clause.

Japan's major goal at the peace conference was to retain control of the Shantung Peninsula and Germany's former colonies in the Pacific Ocean. It did not achieve all of its goals.

- Japan retained control of the Shantung Peninsula for only a few years, after China's demand for its return was supported by the USA.
- The League of Nations established **mandates** for former colonies and territories of the defeated powers.
- Japan received the mandate of Germany's Pacific territories, allowing it to administer these territories but not to **annex** them.

Despite not achieving all of its goals at the Paris Peace Conference, there was no doubt that Japan had become the major power in Asia. In a few short years, it had:

- defeated Russia in the Russo-Japanese War
- annexed Korea
- leased important ports and territories in China
- defeated German forces in Asia
- negotiated with the world's major powers in shaping the post-war world.

To secure these new territories and expand its power and influence, Japan instituted **conscription** and increased the size of its navy.

IDENTIFYING RELEVANT CONTENT

Use Source D to identify words and phrases that indicate racist beliefs. Highlight or underline the words and phrases.

SOURCE D

Excerpt from a 'Letter from US President Theodore Roosevelt to Senator Knox', 1909, Papers of Theodore Roosevelt, Library of Congress, Washington, DC, USA. Senator Knox became Secretary of State (Minister of Foreign Affairs) in 1909 for President Taft.

But with Japan the case is different. She is a most formidable military power. Her people have a peculiar fighting capacity. They are very proud, very warlike, very sensitive, and are influenced by two contradictory feelings; namely, a great self-confidence, both ferocious and conceited, due to their victory over the mighty empire of Russia; and a great touchiness because they would like to be considered as on a full equality with, as one of the brotherhood of, Occidental [European states and the US] nations, and have been bitterly humiliated to find that even their allies, the English, and their friends, the Americans, won't admit them to association and citizenship, as they admit the least advanced or most decadent European peoples. Moreover, Japan's population is increasing rapidly and demands an outlet; and the Japanese labourers, small farmers, and petty traders would, if permitted, flock by the hundred thousand to the United States, Canada, and Australia.

USING OWN KNOWLEDGE

- The last question, question 12, requires students to write an extended response based on all sources given and their own knowledge. This question is worth 9 marks. It is the most valuable question and you should devote the most time to answering it.
- Own knowledge means any knowledge or understanding of a topic not found in the sources provided in the exam booklet.
- One effective method is to use a thematic approach and perspective to structure your own knowledge.

Use the information from the opposite page about the First World War and the Paris Peace Conference to support the idea that racism and perspective contributed to long-term tensions between Japan and the west.

Below is the beginning of a sample extended response to the last question of Paper 1 requiring students to use the sources and their own knowledge. Complete the response using information from the opposite page.

Using the sources and your own knowledge, evaluate the role of racism in causing the Second World War in Asia.

A major factor leading to war between Japan and the west was the effect of racism on the perception of the effects of the First World War and the Paris Peace Conference.

Interwar treaties

Japan and the USA were the most powerful states in the Pacific Ocean after the First World War. Both countries desired security for their territories in the region. Economically, Japan sought and needed good ties with the USA, especially for oil and metals. The USA wanted access to the Chinese market. Japan had significant investments in China requiring military presence due to the unstable political situation in China. Limiting military strengths was important to both countries.

Japan's interwar foreign policy

The foreign policy goals of Japan's military and civilian government were not perfectly aligned. Japan's military wanted to:

- maintain its strength and expand its size
- protect Japan's territorial interests from foreign powers
- add more territory under Japanese control.

The civilian government was concerned with:

- appeasing the military due to its political influence in the cabinet
- economic pressures that could result from enlarging the military
- maintaining good economic relations with the USA and European powers
- not provoking the USA, Britain or other European powers.

Foreign Minister **Kijūrō Shidehara** developed a policy that allowed the military to expand and reassured foreign powers. This policy came to be known as Shidehara Diplomacy and lasted until 1931.

Washington Naval Conference and treaties 1921–2

The Washington Naval Conference sought to limit the size of navies. In the Five-Power Treaty, also known as the Washington Naval Treaty, the USA, Britain and Japan agreed to:

- stop building battleships for ten years
- scrap some **capital ships**
- a 5 : 5 : 3 ratio of capital ships: for every five capital ships for the USA and Britain, Japan was allowed three
- limit the building of fortifications in the Pacific to only Pearl Harbor, Hawaii for the USA.

In the Four-Power Treaty, Britain, France, the USA and Japan agreed to respect each other's territories. In the Nine-Power Treaty, Japan agreed to remove its military from the Shantung Peninsula.

Japan's military was not pleased with these treaties. Japan's civilian government was satisfied because the agreements limited spending during economic troubles and provided a basis for good relations with western powers.

London Naval Conference 1930

The London Naval Conference was designed to review the earlier naval agreements. Japan wanted a better ratio for its capital ships. A compromise allowed Japan to increase its ratio of battleships to 69.75%, but to retain a 60% ratio for cruisers. The military's threat of a political crisis failed. Ultranationalists hated the agreement and one of them assassinated Japan's prime minister.

Military expansion

After restrictions on military spending for most of the 1920s, political pressure grew to increase the size of the military and for expansion to gain natural resources. Japan turned to China.

Increased spending

Japan's navy was limited by several treaties. Its army was not. As the military increased its political power in Japan, it was able to increase the size of the army. To address the economic crisis of the **Great Depression**, the government used military spending to stimulate the economy. Japan's military might greatly increased.

EXAMINING A SOURCE'S PURPOSE

- Question 10 of Paper 1 requires students to evaluate the value and limitations of a source based on its origin, purpose and content. The question is worth 4 marks.
- The purpose of a source refers to why the author created the source.
- Knowing why a source was created can provide some insight into what kind of information was included and what kind of information may have been omitted.
- It also might give an indication to the perspective of the author.

Below is the description of a source, Source E, that refers to the Washington Naval Conference of 1921–2.

SOURCE E

Excerpt from *The Autobiography of Ozaki Yukio: The Struggle for Constitutional Government in Japan* by Ozaki Yukio, published by Princeton University Press, Princeton, New Jersey, USA, 2001, pp. 341–2. Ozaki was a member of Japan's House of Representatives from 1889 to 1953. The following passage concerns the treaties signed by Japan at the Washington Naval Conference, 1921–2.

13 Source E is an autobiography. What is the purpose of an autobiography?

14 How might the purpose of an autobiography influence the information Ozaki Yukio included in his comments about the Washington Naval Conference, 1921–2?

15 How might the purpose of an autobiography influence the information Ozaki Yukio did not include in his comments about the Washington Naval Conference, 1921–2?

CONNECTING PURPOSE TO CONTENT

As mentioned above, the purpose of a source can influence the content included in the source. Use Source F to answer the questions designed to connect purpose to content.

SOURCE F

Extract from a policy statement, 'A Rapprochement with China', delivered by Foreign Minister Kijūrō Shidehara to the Japanese Diet on 21 January 1930 in *Sources of Japanese Tradition*, Second Edition, Volume Two: 1600 to 2000, Abridged, Part Two: 1880 to 2000, compiled by William Theodore de Bary, Carol Gluck and Arthur E. Tiedemann, published by Columbia University Press, New York, USA, 2006, pp. 209–10.

If … one takes a broader view of the future well-being of both China and Japan, one will be satisfied that there is no other course open to the two nations than to pursue the path of mutual accord and cooperation in all their relations, political and economic. Their real and lasting interests, which in no way conflict but have much in common with each other, ought to be a significant assurance of their growing rapprochement. If the Chinese people awaken to these facts and show themselves responsive to the policy so outlined, nothing will more conduce to the mutual welfare of both nations. Should they, on the contrary, fail to understand us and seek trouble with us, we can at least rest assured of our strong position in the public opinion of the world.

16 Why would Shidehara give a policy statement to the Diet?

17 How does his purpose affect the contents of his statement?

18 Refer to the information from the opposite page and list key knowledge not included in this policy statement.

Economic and political issues

Revised ▢

Economics had a great influence on Japanese foreign policy during a period of economic instability. Japan experienced periods of growth followed by periods of decline. **Monopolies** expanded their control of the economy as a result of this instability. Economic instability affected political instability.

▢ Industrialization and foreign policy

Industrialization meant wealth and security for those industrialized countries. Those countries, such as China, that failed to industrialize were weak. They could not protect themselves from imperial powers.

Japan's industrial growth from the late nineteenth century to the end of the First World War was astonishing. In a short time, it went from a feudal country to a world power. Modern technology and a modern economy allowed Japan to export goods throughout the Pacific region.

▢ *Zaibatsu*

Zaibatsu were huge corporations, monopolies, owned by families with vast influence in multiple industries. By 1918, eight *zaibatsu* controlled twenty per cent of manufacturing, mining and trade.

The economic troubles of the late 1920s and the Great Depression allowed them to get larger as smaller businesses failed. The *zaibatsu* turned economic power into political power in the Diet, allowing them to shape economic policies. Soon they turned to the military for an ally and became important players in Japanese militarism.

▢ Social stress and employment

Industrialization caused great social stress. From the First World War to the Great Depression, Japan experienced cycles of boom with high employment and busts with massive unemployment.

- Japan's economy grew during the First World War.
- By 1920, western nations were trading again and Japan's economy suffered, causing widespread unemployment.
- Rebuilding efforts after an earthquake and fire devastated Tokyo in 1923 caused the economy and jobs to swell.
- Prosperity was short lived as bank failures helped collapse the economy in 1927, creating massive unemployment.
- The Great Depression occurred.

▢ The Great Depression

The Great Depression began in 1929 and plunged the world into economic troubles. In an effort to protect domestic economies, most countries resorted to **trade barriers** on foreign imports. Japan's economy suffered because it relied on exports, especially to the USA.

- Japan's **gross national product (GNP)** fell by twenty per cent by 1931.
- The Tokyo Stock Market lost 50% of its value.
- Exports decreased by over 40%.
- About half of small- and medium-sized businesses closed.
- Unemployment rose substantially.

Economic hardship caused political unrest, including strikes, riots and demands for a new form of government. The *zaibatsu*, however, were able to increase their share of the market with the failure of smaller businesses.

The government tried to solve the crisis, including plans to send Japanese workers to Manchuria. By 1936, there had been little success. The Finance Minister was assassinated in 1936. He was replaced by a military appointee. The military began to dominate the government by:

- increasing military spending to modernize and expand the military
- seeking new territory to solve the natural resources problem, such as lack of iron, coal and oil
- formulating an expansionist policy that meant more war and the need for a war economy.

EVALUATE A SOURCE USING ORIGIN, PURPOSE, CONTENT, VALUE, LIMITATIONS

- Question 10 of Paper 1 requires students to evaluate the value and limitations of a source based on its origin, purpose and content. This question is worth 4 marks.
- The demand of the question is to evaluate the value and limitation of a source. Full marks cannot be achieved without evaluating value and limitation.
- To do this, connect value and limitation by referring to origin, purpose and/or content in the evaluation. When writing about a value or limitation be sure to add information about origin, purpose and/or content in the same sentence. Listing information about origin, purpose and content cannot attain full marks.
- It is important to use the terms origin, purpose, content, value and limitation in the response. Using these terms makes it easier to ensure that a response has fully addressed the question and makes it easier for an examiner to identify that all the demands of the question have been addressed.

With reference to its origin, purpose and content, evaluate the value and limitations of Source G, below, for a historian studying economic and political issues from the First World War to 1936 on Japan's road to war.

SOURCE G

Excerpt from *Fifty Years of Light and Dark: The Hirohito Era* by the staff of the *Mainichi Daily News*, The Mainichi Newspapers, Tokyo, Japan, 1975, p. 25. *Mainichi Shimbun* or *Daily News*, has been published since 1872 and is one of the largest media companies in Japan.

[During the start of the Great Depression], the number of banks shrank from 1,300 to some 700. Big banks, including Mitsui, Mitsubishi, Sumitomo, Daiichi and Yasuda, strengthened their oligopolistic hold on Japan's economy. The formidable Zaibatsu were steadily solidifying their financial grip on the nation's economic world.

Suffering under persistent depression, the public found its target of patriotic resentment in the large-scale 'buy dollar' policy pursued by Zaibatsu, especially Mitsui, in the second half of 1931. The powerful industrial-financial concern, anticipating the impending ban on gold export, went ahead to buy US dollars on a grand scale ... But patriots and patriotically-inclined press called the Zaibatsu managers 'traitors of the nation' who had handed out national currencies en masse 'in exchange for white men's money.' The government collapsed in the face of public outbursts ...

Origin	Value
• Who created the source?	• What does this source let me know about the topic under study?
• When was it created?	• Does the source allow for a general understanding?
• What type of source is it?	• Does the source tell me only about one perspective?
– speech, letter, diary, government document, and so on	• How does knowing the origin and purpose help me determine value?
– primary or secondary	
• Where was it published?	
• Is there any important information about the author that may be useful?	
– historian, author's position, historical significance, and so on	

Purpose	Limitation
• Why was the source created?	• What does this source not let me know about the topic under study?
• What was the author hoping to do by creating this source?	• If it is from a limited perspective, what does it not help me understand?
• Who is the intended audience?	• How does knowing the origin and purpose help me determine limitations?
• Based on the above questions:	
– is this what the author truly believes?	
– is it a partially true belief?	
– is it created for a goal(s) other than recording some truth?	

Domestic instability and foreign affairs

The economic crisis caused political instability. The governing system from the Meiji Constitution was losing legitimacy. Japan's interests in Manchuria and calls for expansion meant that foreign policy and domestic policy were closely tied together.

Instability: domestic

Japan's governing system was complex and contained numerous structural conflicts:

- the military had direct access to the Emperor
- the cabinet was solely responsible to the Emperor
- policies required unanimous approval by ministers to be enacted
- the House of Representatives controlled taxes, budgets and funding
- the House of Peers contained many former ministers who often acted independently
- the Privy Council, composed of *genrō*, had direct access to the Emperor and could veto any government proposals.

The increasing number of political parties added even more demands, making compromise even harder. The ultimate authority of the Emperor became even more important. The Great Depression increased the problems of government, bringing even more political instability to Japan.

Communism

Communism's call for the overthrow of government and equality for all held great appeal for many. The Peace Protection Law of 1925 (amended in 1928) allowed for the arrest and execution of anyone wanting to change the government system. Perhaps more importantly, the anti-communist policy acted as opposition to the Soviet Union, the world's only communist state. The Soviet Union bordered Korea and Manchuria, making it a threat to Japanese interests in Asia.

The Shōwa Restoration

A conservative movement grew calling for full power be given to the **Shōwa Emperor**. Direct rule for the Shōwa Emperor would eliminate the problems of government. The idea especially appealed to rural farmers, most with no prospects for a decent life. They joined the military, where they became a base for powerful conservative forces. They supported young, ultranationalist officers who also believed in the Shōwa Restoration.

Military factions

Japan's military was internally divided into two factions: one faction wanted reform; the other faction wanted direct rule from the Emperor.

The **Tōseiha** wanted reform; it would:

- ally with the *zaibatsu* and government officials
- suppress political parties
- tightly control the economy
- prepare for eventual **total war** with China and, perhaps, other states.

The radical faction desired complete, direct rule by the Emperor; it wanted:

- complete destruction of political parties and the *zaibatsu*
- to destroy the corrupt and incompetent governing system
- to eliminate communists and **socialists**
- war with the Soviet Union.

The radical faction attempted several *coups d'état* between 1931 and 1936. Several high-ranking officials and *zaibatsu* leaders were assassinated during these attempted *coups d'état*.

The Tōseiha gained the support of the Emperor, the Privy Council, the cabinet, the Diet and the *zaibatsu*. The Tōseiha now controlled the government. It reorganized the economy, suppressed dissent, and expanded military budgets and war (but avoided conflict with the Soviet Union).

The military came to dominate Japan's government. Between 1932 and December 1941, Japan had nine different prime ministers. Six of the prime ministers were army generals or navy admirals.

COMPARING SOURCES

- Question 11 of Paper 1 requires students to compare and contrast two sources. The question is worth 6 marks.
- The comparing and contrasting of the sources should focus on the content of the sources.
- When comparing sources, students should identify and explain similarities in content found in the sources.
- Three similarities and three differences are needed to achieve full marks for the comparing portion of this question.
- You should spend about fifteen minutes answering this question.

For this activity, use Sources H and I to complete the table below.

	Source H	Source I	Explanation
Similarity 1			
Similarity 2			
Similarity 3			

SOURCE H

Excerpt from *Emperor Hirohito and His Chief Aide-de-Camp: The Honjō Diary, 1933–36* by Honjō Shigeru, translated by Mikiso Hane, published by University of Tokyo Press, Tokyo, Japan, 1982, p. 173. Honjō was head of the Kwantung Army of Japan from 1931 to 1932 and later served as the military's liaison with Japan's Emperor until 1936. Mikiso Hane was an internationally renowned historian on Japanese history and was a professor at Knox College in the USA from 1961 to 1992.

March 2 [1936]: His Majesty [Emperor Hirohito] summoned me after 11:00 a.m. and said, 'Soon [*genrō*] Saionji will come to the capital, and a new cabinet must be chosen. It seems that the army's conditions concerning cabinet members continue to be rigid. It appears to be aggressive about policy matters too. Unless the military's wishes are taken into consideration, another incident like the recent [26 February *coup d'état* attempt] affair might break out again. For this reason, I would like to take the army's desires into consideration, but excessively radical changes would conflict with the state of society as a whole. We must act with extreme caution. I, too, am pulled into two directions about this. The military may justifiably demand a strong national defense program, but it steps out of bounds when it moves into the arena of national economy and calls for the distribution of wealth. When you confer with the high-ranking army officers you should keep this in mind.'

SOURCE I

Excerpt from *The Age of Hirohito: In Search of Modern Japan* by Daikichi Irokawa, published by The Free Press, New York, USA, 1995, p. 13. The author is a professor at Tokyo Kenzai University and has published books on Japanese history and culture in the nineteenth and twentieth centuries.

By cleverly making use of right-wing [Kōdōha] power in the military and … political arenas but keeping a safe distance from the extreme rightists, a group of pragmatic military officers known as Tōseiha and government bureaucrats linked with the new and old *zaibatsu* then seeking to make the Asian continent their base of operations. This faction set out to free Japan from economic depression by a course of aggression.

To further their objectives, they assassinated Zhang Zuolin, and in the same year imprisoned several thousand communists and labor leaders.

CONTRASTING SOURCES

- Question 11 of Paper 1 requires students to compare and contrast two sources. The question is worth 6 marks.
- The comparing and contrasting of the sources should focus on the content of the sources.
- When contrasting sources, students should identify and explain differences in content found in the sources.
- Three similarities and three differences are needed to achieve full marks for the comparing portion of this question.
- You should spend about fifteen minutes answering this question.

For this activity, use Sources H and I above to complete the table below.

	Source H	Source I	Explanation
Difference 1			
Difference 2			
Difference 3			

Instability: foreign affairs

Political instability and a weak national government in China made the country vulnerable to a foreign power.

The Warlord Era

Between 1918 and 1928, regional warlords controlled China and fought one another for power and territory. Zhang Zuolin, warlord in Manchuria and Inner Mongolia, eventually became the most powerful warlord.

Manchuria

Zhang Zuolin's powerful army brought stability to Manchuria, allowing it to declare independence in 1922. The Japanese government supported Zhang, because he permitted Japan to develop its economic interests in Manchuria. Japan's Kwantung Army officers, many of whom were members of the radical faction Kōdōha, however, saw his autonomy and large army as a threat. Kwantung Army officers assassinated Zhang in 1928. They were seen as nationalistic heroes in Japan and not punished for their insubordination.

Southern China and the end of the warlords

The Kuomintang (KMT) used Chinese nationalism and anti-foreign sentiment to unite various factions in southern China. Strengthened by its support of the anti-foreign movement and an alliance with Chinese Communist Party (CCP), the KMT was strong enough to defeat the warlords in a military campaign called the Northern Expedition. During the campaign, the KMT turned on its communist allies in what eventually would become a civil war. The success of the KMT led Zhang's son and also his successor to bring Manchuria back into a united China.

A newly united China

Chiang Kai-shek, head of the KMT, became China's Director of the State Council, the equivalent of President. Economic and political reorganization strengthened China despite the destruction and casualties from the Northern Expedition. However, the KMT's attack on the CCP meant the loss of a potential ally in the Soviet Union, which supported the CCP.

Japan's foreign policy towards China up to 1931

From the First World War to 1927, Japan's foreign policy had been shaped by Shidehara Diplomacy that emphasized:

- international diplomacy and negotiations
- reluctance to antagonize the USA or China
- implementing treaties that allowed Japanese troops to protect Japanese interests in Manchuria and several port cities.

The success of Chiang Kai-shek and the KMT changed Japan's policy beginning in 1927 to the Positive Policy. As a result, Japan:

- treated Manchuria as a special case
- hoped to prevent a Chinese invasion of Manchuria
- sent troops to occupy the Shantung Peninsula
- supported the warlord Zhang Zuolin in Manchuria
- believed that the international community's policies aimed to weaken Japan in Manchuria
- considered foreign powers incapable of understanding Japan's needs and special mission in Asia.

The elite Kwantung Army was stationed in the Liaodong Peninsula to protect Japan's interests there as well as the border of Korea, Japan's colony. With a newly united China, more troops reinforced the Kwantung Army. This strengthened the conviction among the Kwantung Army officers that their beliefs regarding Manchuria were crucial to Japan's security and needs. Worried about future insubordination, Japan's government decided to replace the Kwantung Army leadership. Hours before this could happen, the Manchurian Crisis occurred.

SUMMARIZING A SOURCE

- Question 12 of Paper 1 requires students to integrate knowledge from four sources and their own understanding in response to a question about a topic from one of the case studies in The move to global war.
- A successful response requires students to integrate summaries of sources.
- A good summary is based on the main ideas of a source. The main idea of a source can be identified using relevant content or identifying how relevant content is connected by a bigger idea or concept.
- You should spend 30–35 minutes answering the question. It is recommended that the first five to eight minutes be used to outline your response. You should spend the last 25 minutes writing the essay.

Answer the questions below about Source J. After answering the questions, write a one- or two-sentence summary of Source J.

SOURCE J

Excerpt from *Emperor Hirohito and Shōwa Japan: A Political Biography* by Stephen S. Large, published by Routledge, New York, USA, 1992, pp. 35–6. Large is a historian whose books have concentrated on biographies of Japan's recent emperors and socialist politics in Japan in the early twentieth century.

The Emperor, Saionji and Shidehara were eager to prevent any further conflict in north China which might spill over into Japan's sphere of influence in south Manchuria. [Prime Minister] Tanaka, it must be said, fully agreed with this and accordingly urged Chang Tso-lin [Zhang Zuolin] to evacuate the region and retire to Manchuria, his original power base, lest [he] become embroiled in a military confrontation with Chiang Kai-shek's Nationalist [KMT] forces in north China. Tanaka believed that Chang's forces and Japanese interests could co-exist in Manchuria.

But this was not the view of the Kwantung Army, which pressed Tanaka to authorize at least the disarming of Chang's troops as he moved north. When Tanaka refused, Colonel Kōmoto Daisaku, a staff officer in the Kwantung Army, and several associates, plotted Chang's assassination which they would attribute to Chinese 'bandits'. They hoped that this course of action would stiffen the Japanese government's resolve to render Japan's position in Manchuria impregnable. In this, they were to be disappointed.

19 What was the biggest concern Japan's government had about north China?
20 What did the Japanese government believe was possible in Manchuria between Japan and Chang Tso-lin?
21 What motivated the Kwantung Army's actions?
22 What does the source suggest about the relationship between the Japanese government and the radical factions in the Japanese military?

Use the space below to write your summary of Source J.

INTEGRATING KNOWLEDGE AND SOURCES

Using Sources A–J found in Chapter 1, identify relevant content to help answer the question:

Examine the causes of Japanese expansion up to 1931.

Use the table below to record a brief summary of the relevant content from each source.

Source	Brief summary		Source	Brief summary
Source A			Source F	
Source B			Source G	
Source C			Source H	
Source D			Source I	
Source E			Source J	

Source booklet

Read Sources A–D below and answer questions 9–12 in the accompanying question paper.

SOURCE A

Excerpt from *Emperor Hirohito and His Chief Aide-de-Camp: The Honjō Diary, 1933–36* by Honjō Shigeru, translated by Mikiso Hane, published by University of Tokyo Press, Tokyo, Japan, 1982, p. 173. Honjō was head of the Kwantung Army of Japan from 1931 to 1932 and later served as the military's liaison with Japan's Emperor until 1936. Mikiso Hane was an internationally renowned historian on Japanese history and was a professor at Knox College in the USA from 1961 to 1992.

[Ultranationalist ideologist] Ōkawa Shūmei placed the emperor system at the core of his thinking, regarding it as the source of morality and religion. He emphasized the 'way of the Japanese' and the 'Japanese Spirit', which embodies 'statism, idealism, the principle of combat and spirituality.' 'The Japanese spirit,' in Ōkawa's opinion was incompatible with the 'Anglo-American democratic spirit which is the product of individualism, utilitarianism, hedonism, and materialism.' A second Restoration was needed, Ōkawa asserted, to free people from the oppression of materialism and unite the people and the Emperor. The uniqueness of Japan entitled it to become the leader of Asia …

SOURCE B

A woodblock print titled *In the Battle of Nanshan, Lieutenant Shibakawa Matasaburi Led His Men Holding up a Rising Sun War Fan* by Getsuzo, 1904. Located at MIT Visualizing Cultures, Massachusetts Institute of Technology, Cambridge, Massachusetts, USA.

SOURCE C

Excerpt from *The Imperial Rescript on Education* by the Roy Rosenzweig Center for History and New Media, located at *Children and Youth in History*. https://chnm.gmu.edu/cyh/primary-sources/136

Know ye [you], Our Subjects:

Our Imperial Ancestors have founded Our [the Meiji Emperor's] Empire on a basis broad and everlasting, and have deeply and firmly implanted virtue; Our subjects ever united in loyalty and filial piety [respect for elders and those in authority] have from generation to generation illustrated the beauty thereof. This is the glory of the fundamental character of Our Empire, and herein also lies the source of Our education, Ye, Our Subjects, be filial to your parents, affectionate to your brothers and sisters; as husbands and wives be harmonious, as friends true; bear yourselves in modesty and moderation; extend your benevolence to all; pursue learning and cultivate arts, and thereby develop intellectual faculties and perfect moral powers; furthermore, advance public good and promote common interests; always respect the Constitution and observe the laws; should emergency arise, offer yourselves courageously to the State; and thus guard and maintain prosperity of Our Imperial state; and thus guard and maintain the prosperity of Our Imperial Throne coeval with heaven and earth (for as long as heaven and earth exist), So shall ye not only be Our good and faithful subjects, but render illustrious the best traditions of your forefathers.

The way here set forth is indeed the teaching bequeathed by Our Imperial Ancestors, to be observed alike by Their Descendants and the subjects, infallible for all ages and true in all places. It is Our wish to lay it to heart in all reverence, in common with you, Our subjects, that we may all attain to the same virtue.

SOURCE D

Excerpt from a 'Letter from US President Theodore Roosevelt to Senator Knox', 1909, Papers of Theodore Roosevelt, Library of Congress, Washington, DC, USA. Roosevelt negotiated the Treaty of Portsmouth that resolved the Russo-Japanese War in 1905. Senator Knox became US Secretary of State (Minister of Foreign Affairs) in 1909 for US President Taft.

But with Japan the case is different. She is a most formidable military power. Her people have peculiar fighting capacity. They are very proud, very warlike, very sensitive, and are influenced by two contradictory feelings; namely, a great self-confidence, both ferocious and conceited, due to their victory over the mighty empire of Russia; and a great touchiness because they would like to be considered as on a full equality with, as one of the brotherhood of, Occidental [European states and the US] nations, and have been bitterly humiliated to find that even their allies, the English, and their friends, the Americans, won't admit them to association and citizenship, as they admit the least advanced or most decadent European peoples. Moreover, Japan's population is increasing rapidly and demands an outlet; and the Japanese laborers, small farmers, and petty traders would, if permitted, flock by the hundred thousand into the United States, Canada, and Australia.

Sample questions and answers

Below are sample answers. Read them and the comments around them.

9a According to Source A, what were key results of ultranationalist belief in Japan?

> Ultranationalist belief placed the emperor system at the core of thinking because it was the source of morality and religion.
>
> A second Restoration was needed to free Japan from harmful Anglo-American beliefs.
>
> Ultranationalists believed in statism, idealism, the idea of combat and spirituality.

This is a good example of using the text itself to help show understanding of the question as much of the sentence comes directly from the text. A slight edit using the word 'because' simplifies the meaning of the text.

This response describes components of ultranationalist belief, not what they result in. Therefore, it does not address the demands of the question and cannot achieve any marks for the response.

2/3. The first two sentences identify the relevant content that addresses the demands of the question: 'key result of ultranationalist belief'. The last sentence does not address a 'key result of ultranationalist belief'. A third mark could be attained by using the key belief, using the last sentence from the source about Japan being unique and becoming the leading nation in Asia.

This is a good example of summarizing the text with focus on 'key result of ultranationalist belief' with information from the text instead of listing information.

9b What is the message conveyed in Source B?

> The print emphasizes nationalism and militarism by portraying Lieutenant Shibakawa Matasaburi as brave, heroic and winning glory for himself and Japan by defeating Russia in the Russo-Japanese War.
>
> By holding a Rising Sun War fan, Lieutenant Shibakawa Matasaburi shows the important values of devotion and loyalty to his country as well as his willingness to risk his life in order to make Japan a major power by defeating Russia.

2/2. This response gets full marks. It makes two observations about the message of the illustration. The observations explain the meanings of the images and text on it by connecting them to nationalism, militarism and loyalty to the Emperor and to Japan. It does not simply describe the image.

10 With reference to its origin, purpose and content, evaluate the value and limitations of Source C for a historian studying nationalism and militarism on Japan's road to war.

Source C <u>originates</u> from an official government statement called The Imperial Rescript created in 1890, excerpted by the Roy Rosenzweig Center for History and New Media and located at the website Children and Youth in History. The <u>purpose</u> of the rescript was to establish official government policy on what should be taught in Japanese schools such as loyalty, duty to the Emperor and country, respecting laws and protecting the Emperor and Japan. The source has <u>value</u> because as a government document and rescript its purpose was to establish the values Japanese schools had to teach students. It is also <u>valuable</u> because these values listed in the source's <u>content</u> show how nationalism was partially shaped by devotion and loyalty to the Emperor and to Japan. The source is <u>limited</u> because it was created in 1890, long before the Second World War began, and because it focuses on education and children, not specifically on nationalism or militarism. It also is <u>limited</u> because the content does not show how nationalism led to war, and it does not mention militarism, even though the idea of guarding the state is a key value of militarism.

This is a good start, because it immediately begins to address the demands of the question starting with origin, which is made clear with the underline.

The response wastes no words and immediately proceeds in the next sentence to address the purpose of the source, again underlining the word 'purpose' for emphasis.

A second sentence on value, using and underlining the word 'valuable', is made by connecting value to content. This sentence means the response has connected value to origin, purpose and content, making it a thorough evaluation.

The next sentence quickly states that it will be about value and connects the value to the purpose of the source, even using the word purpose to make a clear connection. It also refers to origin with the phrase 'as a government document'.

The sentence on purpose also contains a brief summary of content of the source.

The final sentence completes the highly focused response by connecting content in relation to the scope of the question as a limitation.

The first limitation connects to origin with reference to the date it was created, showing the source cannot explain many years of the context of the question. The reference to education and children connects the limitation to the source's origin.

4/4. This response gets full marks because it addresses every demand of the question: origin, purpose, content, value and limitation. These are easy to identify because those terms were used and underlined in the response. This makes it easy for the examiner to identify them and for the student to guarantee they have all been used in the response. Every sentence addresses origin, purpose, content, value and/or content, making it a highly focused response. Most importantly, the value and limitations are explained and connected to origin, purpose and/or content.

11 Compare and contrast what Source A and Source D state about Japanese nationalism.

Both Source A and Source D remark on Japan's militaristic nature, with Source A referring to the Japanese Way's principle of combat and Source D stating that Japan is a formidable military power and its people possess a peculiar fighting capacity. Source A references tensions between Japan and Anglo-American values. Similarly Source D identifies tensions arising from Japan's humiliation by the English and Americans. Source D claims that Japan believes it is equal to the west or occidental nations, so does Source A when it states Japan should be a leader in Asia just as America and Britain are leaders in their regions and in their colonial territories.

Theodore Roosevelt (Source D) writes in the context of foreign relations. On the other hand, Honjō Shigeru (Source A) makes his observation in the context of domestic Japanese politics. Source A rejects western values including materialism, but Source D implies that Japanese will emigrate to USA, Canada and Australia because they want better economic opportunities that bring material benefits. Source D has racist overtones, citing the Japanese as possessing touchiness, and implies that Japan's aspirations are unrealistic whereas Source A is very proud of the Japanese Way and people.

> This is a good start with an immediate identification of similarity with the beginning phrase '[b]oth Source A and Source D …'

> This is a good combination of summary, 'remark on Japan's militaristic nature' and key words from the sentence such as 'Japanese Way's principle of combat'.

> The comparison paragraph ends with a solid interpretation of both sources regarding Japan's stature related to the west.

The contrasting section begins with a good example of differences in context in foreign relations contrasted with domestic politics and the use of parenthetical reference to identify sources.

Throughout the response, there is excellent use of appropriate language that builds linkage such as 'similarly', 'on the other hand' and other words such as 'both', 'but', 'whereas'.

5/6. This is a strong response, especially the comparison section. Separating the paragraphs into comparing and contrasting topics brings clarity to the answer. It also helps the writer stay focused and to ensure that the response is complete. The response does a good job of using direct quotes, paraphrases and summaries of the sources. The structure of sentences with both sources used in a single sentence or in consecutive sentences also provides focus and clarity. The final sentence in the contrasting paragraph could be considered to be a similarity focused on racist attitudes.

12 Using the sources and your own knowledge, discuss the causes of Japanese expansion on the road to war up to 1931.

A number of factors caused Japanese expansion up to 1931 including Japanese nationalism and militarism; militarism and foreign policy; economic and political issues; and domestic instability and foreign affairs. Source C describes the character of education that helped shape the nature of nationalism and militarism in Japan. It taught that the Emperor was divine and that all Japanese owed loyalty and obedience to him. It also created a sense of duty to courageously defend the Emperor and Japan even if it meant self-sacrifice. For some Japanese, the sense of nationalism became radical. They believed Japan had a special mission because the Emperor was divine, Japan had never been colonized, and had defeated Russia in the Russo-Japanese War. Source A called this the 'way of the Japanese' and the 'Japanese spirit'. Therefore, Japan should become the leader of Asia.

Japan's long tradition of militarism became tied to nationalism and both influenced Japan's foreign policy. Beginning with Korea in the late-1800s, Japan began expanding its

> Starting with an organization statement gives clarity to the student and to the examiner.

> Using brief quotes of key phrases from sources is highly effective.

influence in Asia. Its interest in Korea brought conflict with China, which had influence over Korea for centuries. These tensions led to the first Sino-Japanese War. Because of the Meiji modernization programme, Japan had a modern military and easily defeated China. However, western interference from the Tripartite Intervention meant Japan lost Port Arthur to the Russians and other advantages they had gained from their victory. Tensions between Russia and Japan continued to grow until they went to war in the Russo-Japanese War. Japanese soldiers like Lieutenant Shibakawa Matasaburi, seen in Source B, fulfilled their duty to the Emperor as they were taught by the ideals of Source C, as well as their sense of nationalism seen in his fan with the Rising Sun emblem. As a result of its victory, Japan believed it was equal to the western powers, as stated by Theodore Roosevelt in Source D. Roosevelt's letter, however, indicates that racism prevented westerners from seeing the Japanese as equals. The terms of the Paris Peace Treaties following the First World War and the naval treaties reinforced Japan's frustration at what they believed was unfair treatment by the west.

> It is acceptable to incorporate a significant amount of own knowledge without reference to a source.

> Connecting knowledge from two sources to support one claim is another effective technique.

Japan's industrialization helped it create a modern military, but it required a lot of natural resources not found in Japan. The need for natural resources was a major factor influencing Japan's expansion, especially its actions in Manchuria with its rich resources and land. The problems of the Great Depression deepened Japan's interest in Manchuria as a place to relocate its many unemployed workers and farmers. As a leader of Asia, as stated in Source A, it was only natural for Japan to use Manchuria.

> Each paragraph focuses on only one topic and incorporates both source and own knowledge.

Not all tensions leading to expansion resulted from foreign policy. The growth of radical nationalism, known as ultranationalism, and the military's increasing political power in domestic politics also caused expansion. Ultranationalists and some in the military, especially those who were ultranationalist, became impatient with democracy and the government's caution. Source A shows this with its call for a 'second Restoration' or Shōwa Restoration. They wanted the Showa Emperor to rule directly, which would benefit the military who by law could communicate directly with the Emperor. When they became frustrated, ultranationalists and military officers sometimes acted on their own such as the assassination of the Chinese warlord of Manchuria. They hoped the assassination would create problems in Manchuria requiring Japan to increase their military there and to increase Japan's control of Manchuria.

> Full development of ultranationalism and ultranationalists shows depth of historical knowledge and understanding.

Japanese nationalism and militarism had a great influence on foreign policy, foreign affairs and domestic politics leading to Japan's expansion up to 1931. From Japan's first expansion into Korea through war with Russia, growing tensions with the west, and the political and economic impact of the Great Depression, Japan sought answers to aims and goals in expansion.

> The conclusion summarizes the argument and answers the demands of the question.

9/9. This is a strong response that uses all sources and most of them more than once and in different ways. The organization provides clarity, structured elements and balance to the response. It uses the subheadings in Chapter 1 as an organizing tool. Subheadings will not work for every essay question, but they provide guidance for students having difficulty in organizing their revision notes. The response does not rely only on the sources for knowledge and understanding. It integrates a great deal of own knowledge. The use of significant own knowledge allows for a complete addressing of the demands of the question. This is important to score well on question 12. Using only information from the sources will not allow for a full response to the demands of the question. The use of knowledge and understanding from sources and own knowledge in the same sentence is an effective way to integrate knowledge for question 12.

> The command term 'discuss' means to '[o]ffer a considered and balanced review that includes a range of arguments, factors or hypotheses. Opinions or conclusions should be presented clearly and supported by appropriate evidence' (History Guide, first examinations 2017, p. 97)

Exam practice

Now it's your turn to take a mock exam.

Read Sources I–L below and answer questions 9–12 in the accompanying question paper. The sources and questions relate to Case study 1: Japanese expansion in Asia 1931–41.

SOURCE I

Excerpt from *The Age of Hirohito: In Search of Modern Japan* by Daikichi Irokawa, published by The Free Press, New York, USA, 1995, pp. 8–9. The author is a professor at Tokyo Kenzai University and has published books on Japanese history and culture in the nineteenth and twentieth centuries.

Because of such conditions at the lower levels of society, the military could take advantage of the unemployed, impoverished youth and the spiritually exhausted Japanese people to wage its aggressive adventures on the Asian continent. The move to expand the empire also appealed to the struggling financial community, which hoped new markets on the continent would end the Depression, and to an ambitious group of politicians who aspired to a stronger power base.

SOURCE J

A political cartoon by Daniel R. Fitzpatrick, titled 'Piece by Piece', published on 30 July 1937 in the *St. Louis Post-Dispatch*, an American newspaper in St Louis, Missouri, USA. Fitzpatrick was a Pulitzer Prize-winning political cartoonist for the *St. Louis Post-Dispatch* from 1913 to 1958.

PIECE BY PIECE.

SOURCE K

Excerpt from *Emperor Hirohito and His Chief Aide-de-Camp: The Honjō Diary, 1933–36* by Honjō Shigeru, translated by Mikiso Hane, published by University of Tokyo Press, Tokyo, Japan, 1982, p. 173. Honjō was head of the Kwantung Army of Japan from 1931 to 1932 and later served as the military's liaison with Japan's Emperor until 1936. Mikiso Hane was an internationally renowned historian on Japanese history and was professor at Knox College in the USA from 1961 to 1992.

March 2 [1936]: His Majesty [Emperor Hirohito] summoned me after 11:00 a.m. and said, 'Soon [*genrō*] Saionji will come to the capital, and a new cabinet must be chosen. It seems that the army's conditions concerning cabinet members continue to be rigid. It appears to be aggressive about policy matters too. Unless the military's wishes are taken into consideration, another incident like the recent [26 February] affair might break out again. For this reason, I would like to take the army's desires into careful consideration, but excessively radical changes would conflict with the state of society as a whole. We must act with extreme caution. I, too, am pulled in two directions about this. The military may justifiably demand a strong national defense program, but it steps out of bounds when it moves into the area of national economy and calls for the distribution of wealth. When you confer with the high-ranking army officers you should keep this in mind.'

SOURCE L

Excerpt from '1936 coup failed, but rebels killed Japan's "Keynes"' by Jeff Kingston, published in
The Japan Times, **20 February 2016, Tokyo, Japan.** *The Japan Times* **is the largest English-language daily newspaper in Japan. Kingston is the Director of Asian Studies for Temple University and has been a contributing writer to** *The Japan Times* **since 1988.**

This Friday marks the 80th anniversary of the 26th February Incident, a coup staged by young military officers … who resented civilian control of the military, wanted to restore the Emperor to his proper place and purge the polity of corruption and capitalism.

These fanatics were also angry about arms reduction treaties that intruded on the prerogatives of the military … and felt that officers sympathetic to their aims were being sidelined and persecuted. In this context, pending budget cuts were literally a call to arms …

[O]ne of the prime targets was Finance Minister Korekiyo Takahashi, who advocated reduced military spending to promote fiscal consolidation. …

The young officers believed that the problems facing the nation were the result of Japan straying from the essence of *kokutai* (national polity), involving the proper relationship between the Emperor, the people and the state. They called themselves the 'Righteous Army' and adopted the slogan 'Revere the Emperor, Destroy the Traitors.' They drew inspiration from Ikki Kita, a right-wing ideologue who advocated national socialism and a totalitarian state led by the Emperor, and were incensed by widespread poverty in rural areas, which they blamed on the privileged classes. They also believed that the Emperor's closest advisors were deceiving him and usurping his power. The coup aimed for a 'Showa Restoration' that would enable the Emperor to reclaim his authority and purge Japan of Western ideas and those who exploited the people.

9   a   What, according to Source I, was the effect of the Great Depression on the development
         of Japanese expansion?   [3]

     b   What is the message conveyed in Source J?   [2]

10 With reference to its origin, purpose and content, analyse the value and limitations of
    Source L for a historian studying ultranationalism and militarism in Japan from 1930 to 1941. [4]

11 Compare and contrast how Source K and Source L describe the role of the military on
    Japan's government and its policies.   [6]

12 Using the sources and your own knowledge, evaluate the role of ultranationalism and
    militarism on Japan's expansion, 1931–41.   [9]

2 Japan's expansion and the international response

The Manchurian Crisis

By 1931, Japan was heavily invested in Manchuria. It also began to view Manchuria as key to its prosperity and security. Manchuria:

● possessed many resources Japan lacked
● provided access to China's huge market
● was sparsely populated.

The Japanese military and some members of government believed that Manchuria provided a solution to some of Japan's problems, such as being a place where Japan's poor, landless farmers could be settled.

Increasing concern about communism in Japan gave Manchuria even more importance. The Soviet Union and Manchuria shared a long border. If the Japanese military took control in Manchuria, it could:

● be a buffer against a rising communist threat
● act as a deterrent to Soviet intervention in the region
● remove any future conflict between Japan and the Soviet Union far from the home islands of Japan.

At the same time, Chinese construction of rival railways threatened Japan's investment in and revenue from the South Manchurian Railway. Japan's military was already stationed in Manchuria to protect the South Manchurian Railway and other Japanese interests.

If Japan controlled Manchuria, it would benefit Japan's economy and security. The Kwantung Army again acted insubordinately.

■ Events leading to the Manchurian Crisis

On 18 September 1931, the Mukden Incident occurred. A bomb damaged the South Manchurian Railway near the major Manchurian city of Mukden. More importantly, the explosion happened close to a Japanese military garrison that was stationed there to protect the South Manchurian Railway. Japan blamed Chinese troops, but many historians believe that Kwantung Army officers planted the bomb.

The Kwantung Army now had an excuse to seize all of Manchuria. Troops seized the area around Mukden as well as areas around the South Manchurian Railway. They were then joined by a Japanese army based in Korea. By February 1932, almost all of Manchuria was occupied by the Japanese army. Only one province, Jehol, also known as Rehe, remained outside Japanese control. A Chinese army was located in Jehol. Even though the Chinese army in Jehol was much larger than the Japanese one there, the Kuomintang (KMT) government under Chiang Kai-shek ordered its troops not to resist Japan.

Japan declared that it had acted to help Manchuria gain independence from China. A new state was established called Manchukuo, 'Land of the Manchurians' in Japanese. The last Emperor of China, Puyi, a Manchu, was proclaimed the new Emperor of Manchukuo. Other actions were taken to portray Manchukuo's independence, including applications for Manchukuo to participate in the Olympics and to become a member of the League of Nations. Both applications were rejected because Manchukuo was seen as Japan's puppet state.

IDENTIFYING SIGNIFICANT KNOWLEDGE

- Three of the questions for Paper 1 require students to identify and use significant knowledge from a source.
- Significant knowledge refers to knowledge that addresses the demands of a question.

Read the question and Source A below. In the following table, there are knowledge statements. Identify which knowledge statements are significant by placing a tick in the appropriate box. The knowledge statements identified as significant could be used in identifying relevant content, in comparing and contrasting sources, and as knowledge from sources in the open-ended question of Paper 1.

SOURCE A

Excerpt from *The Manchurian Crisis and Japanese Society, 1931–33* by Sandra Wilson, published by Routledge, London, UK, 2002, p. 1. Wilson is a professor of Asian history at Murdoch University, Australia.

On the night of 18 September 1931, a minor explosion occurred on a section of the Japanese-owned South Manchurian Railway near Mukden (now Shenyang) in the north-east of China. Japanese troops stationed in Manchuria since 1905 to protect the railway and its associated operations, moved swiftly and decisively to defend Japan's interests. Meanwhile their leaders loudly asserted to the world that Chinese soldiers were responsible for the explosion, which was branded as only the latest in a series of anti-Japanese 'outrages'. Actually, damage to the railway had been slight, and the 'incident' had in any case been perpetrated not by the Chinese but by Japanese troops, as part of a wider plan to extend power in Manchuria.

1 Identify the knowledge statements determined to be significant for Japanese expansion by placing a tick in the appropriate box.

Knowledge statement	Significant	Not significant
An explosion occurred on 18 September 1931		
Japanese troops had been stationed in Manchuria since 1905		
Japanese troops moved swiftly to defend Japanese interests		
Japan's leaders declared Chinese troops responsible		
Damage to the railway was light		
The incident was part of a wider plan to extend Japanese power in Manchuria		

MARKING AN EVALUATION OF A SOURCE

2 Read the question and sample response below. Determine how many marks out of 4 you would award the response. Remember origin, purpose, content, value and limitation must be addressed. Value and limitation must be connected to origin, purpose or content at least once. Use Source A above in your assessment of the response.

How many marks out of 4 would you award the response below?

> **With reference to its origin, purpose and content, evaluate the value and limitations of Source A, above, for a historian studying Japanese expansion and the international response on Japan's road to war.**
>
> The source is an excerpt from a book about the Manchurian Crisis by a historian. It is valuable because it contains information about the Manchurian Crisis which was one of the reasons for Japan's expansion. Because it is a secondary source, it has less value than a primary source.

▨ Responses to the Manchurian Crisis

Most countries reacted negatively to the Manchurian Crisis, but could do little about it for several reasons:

- the Great Depression
- concerns about the Soviet Union
- or, believing that Manchuria had been saved from the chaos of China.

■ Response: League of Nations

China appealed Japan's occupation of Manchuria to the League of Nations. The League acted cautiously by forming the Lytton Committee. The Lytton Committee acknowledged that Japan had major investments in Manchuria and that Chinese government there had been inefficient and corrupt. However, it also found that:

- Protecting Manchuria was not the reason for Japan's invasion.
- No substantial support for the Manchukuo government existed in Manchuria.
- Most of Manchuria's population was Chinese, not Manchu.

In February 1933, the League of Nations voted to condemn Japan as an aggressor nation. Japan withdrew from the League of Nations with no consequences.

■ Response: China

The Manchurian Crisis caused political change in China. In December 1931, Chiang Kai-shek resigned as premier of China, but remained as head of the military. Chiang would become premier once again in 1935.

On 31 May 1933, China and Japan signed the Tanggu Truce. The truce resulted in:

- recognition that Japan controlled all of Manchuria
- China promising not to try to remove Japan from Manchuria
- establishment of a neutral zone between Japanese-controlled territory and China's territory.

Japan often violated the truce as it continued to enlarge its territory in the region.

Japan's quick victory in Manchuria was greatly aided by Chiang's decision not to resist the Japanese. Chiang:

- realized that the Japanese army was stronger and likely to defeat the Chinese in battle
- may have been more worried about threats to his rule in China such as from the resurgent Chinese Communist Party (CCP)
- battled a northern warlord, who called for fighting the Japanese, throughout most of 1933.

■ Response: USA

After the First World War, the USA entered a period of **semi-isolation**. However, it maintained interests in its **Open Door Policy** towards China. Japan's aggression in Manchuria led to fear that trade in China would be threatened. The USA formulated the **Stimson Doctrine** and refused to recognize the new borders created by Japan's victory in Manchuria. However, it decided against imposing trade restrictions on Japan or Manchuria.

■ Response: Soviet Union

The Soviet Union had little ability to oppose Japan's actions in Manchuria. It was in the midst of economic and social upheaval from its policy of **collectivization** and a resulting famine in the country. In 1935, the Soviet Union, unable to defend the Chinese Eastern Railway (CER) it owned, sold it to Manchukuo in a deal negotiated by Japan.

■ Japan's government after the crisis

The Japanese government's main concern was the insubordination of the Kwantung Army and other army units in Manchuria. It attempted to regain control of the army, which resulted in a series of political conflicts. However, the military refused to cooperate. This conflict set off a chain of events that included the fall of a government and the assassination of a prime minister that led to a naval officer then becoming the new prime minister. As a result, the military was able to influence Japanese government policies even more than previously.

ANALYSING A POLITICAL CARTOON

● Political cartoons are good historical sources that contain a lot of information and messages in a concise source.
● It is important to be able to understand key components of a political cartoon.
● They use symbolism, labels, exaggeration and captions to help convey their messages.

Examine the political cartoon below and then answer the questions that address the various components of a political cartoon.

SOURCE B

A political cartoon titled 'The Doormat' created by David Low, published in the *Evening Standard* newspaper on 19 January 1933. The man kneeling on the right-hand side is British Foreign Secretary John Snow. The man bowing in the doorway is a League of Nations official.

3 The cartoonist uses symbolism to identify the League of Nations and the League Covenant as a doormat (also the caption of the cartoon). What is a doormat? How does this use of symbolism provide meaning about the effectiveness of the League of Nations in the Manchurian Crisis?

4 How is exaggeration used here?

5 What is the meaning of the label on the box ('face-saving outfit') near the British Foreign Secretary?

6 How do exaggeration and the label on the box help create a message?

MIND MAP

The importance of the Manchurian Crisis in Japan's road to war makes it important to know. It may be the topic of a Paper 1 exam. Even if it is not a specific topic, the many connections that can be made to the crisis make it potentially useful as own knowledge for the last question of a Paper 1 exam requiring students to use all the sources and their own knowledge.

Use the information from the opposite page and from Source B to add details to the mind map below.

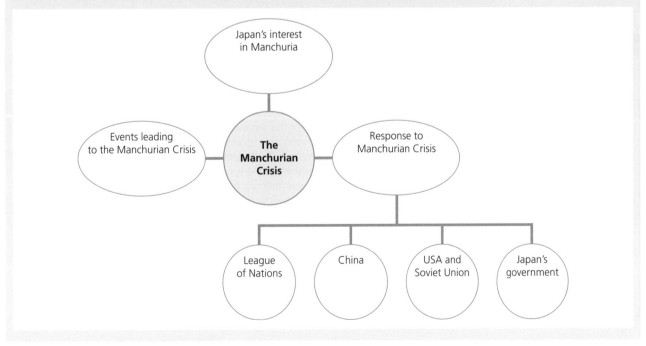

Key debate

Several interpretations of the significance of the Manchurian Crisis exist:

- The road to the Second World War began with the Mukden Incident in 1931, because the weaknesses and failures of the League of Nations contributed to and affected the outcome of the Abyssinian Crisis in 1935–6.
- The crisis revealed a new reality where the **Great Powers** within the League of Nations would not interfere with one another's dealings with smaller states.
- Other historians, such as A.J.P. Taylor, claimed the League of Nations reorganized and became stronger due to the Manchurian Crisis, with the crisis seen as important only after the Second World War.

Regardless of interpretations, several key factors on the road to war emerged as a result of the crisis:

- The League of Nations failed to protect China from Japan.
- Asia moved closer to war because Japan felt secure when it invaded China in 1937.
- The Great Powers did not have the political will or financial ability to intervene in international conflicts.

SOURCE C

Excerpt from *The League of Nations: Its Life and Times 1920–1946* by F.S. Northedge, published by Holmes & Meier, London, UK, 1986, p. 164. Northedge was a professor of international relations at the London School of Economics, UK.

Britain and other great Powers did not worry overmuch about the implications of the Manchurian affair for collective security. As always, they had more immediate questions to think about. In the result, collective security was dealt a blow from which it never fully recovered. The smaller countries were left to conclude that, if the League was to protect them, it would have to be when the great Powers were united against a common enemy, which happened to be victimising a small country. But it was likely as not that the great Powers, so far from joining together to defend the small country would join together to attack it, or to shut their eyes if one of them attacked it. Something like that had happened in the Corfu Incident in 1923, when Italy was sheltered by [being a member of the Conference of Ambassadors]. Japan profited in the same way in the Manchurian affair. Later in the 1930s the European dictators were shielded by sympathisers in the form of states which were supposed to be the very pillars of the League system. And what were the smaller states to do in such situations? They could make their peace with one of the other great Powers in good time, perhaps losing part of their territory in the process of accommodation. Or they could relax their links with the collective system in the hope of diverting from themselves the predatory attention of the great Powers. In either case, the solidity of the League system was bound to be affected as it prepared for the next great challenge. That challenge was not long in coming.

SOURCE D

Excerpt from *The Origins of the Second World War* by A.J.P. Taylor, published by Penguin Books, London, UK, 1991, p. 92. Taylor was a British historian who wrote many books on European history and lectured at many British universities.

The Commission did not reach a simple verdict. It found that most of the Japanese grievances were justified. Japan was not condemned as an aggressor, though she was condemned for resorting to force before all peaceful means of redress were exhausted. The Japanese withdrew in protest from the League of Nations. The Chinese reconciled themselves to the loss of a province which they had not controlled for some years; and in 1933 peace was restored between China and Japan. In later years the Manchurian affair assumed a mythical importance. It was treated as a milestone on the road to war, the first decisive betrayal of the League, especially the British government. In reality, the League, under British leadership, had done what the British thought it was designed to do: it had limited a conflict and brought it, however unsatisfactorily, to an end. Moreover, the Manchurian affair, far from weakening the coercive powers of the League, actually brought them into existence. It was thanks to this affair that the League again on British prompting set up machinery, hitherto lacking, to organize economic sanctions. This machinery, to everyone's misfortune, made possible the League action over Abyssinia in 1935.

COMPARING AND CONTRASTING SOURCES

The following activity is designed to help students identify similarities and differences between sources:

- Similarities and differences should focus on significant knowledge, not basic statements, dates, and so on.
- Differences may identify significant knowledge in one source that is not found in the other source.

Use Source C and Source D on the opposite page. Identify similarities and differences and record them in the table below.

	Source C	Source B	Explanation
Similarity 1			
Similarity 2			
Similarity 3			
Difference 1			
Difference 2			
Difference 3			

WRITING A COMPARE AND CONTRAST RESPONSE

Take the information from the table in the activity above and write a response to the question below. Review the examples of effective sentence structures given below before writing your response.

- A focused response will consist of six statements, one per similarity or difference.
- It also will completely address one demand, compare for example, before addressing the other demand, contrast.

Sample sentence structures for comparing and contrasting sources

Comparing	Contrasting
Both Source C and Source D	Source C emphasizes ... but Source D focuses on ...
Source C identifies ... so does Source D with '... .'	While Source C asserts ... . Source D claims ...
Source D claims ... similarly Source C states ...	Source D examines ... . On the other hand, Source C refers to ...

7　Compare and contrast how Source C and Source D interpret the Manchurian Crisis.

Second Sino-Japanese War 1937–45

In many ways, the Second Sino-Japanese War was an extension of Japan's aggressions beginning with the Manchurian Crisis.

■ Japan expands into China 1935–6

Japan created the China Garrison Army and then used it to occupy part of Charar Province by mid-1935. It then violated the Tanggu Truce when it moved into the neutral zone. The China Garrison Army used the assassination of pro-Japanese newspaper owners to force China to agree to the Umezu–He Agreements on 10 June 1935. This agreement allowed Japan to establish a puppet government in Hebei Province called the East Hebei Autonomous Council.

■ Mengjiang

On 27 June 1935, China signed the Doihara Kenji–Qin Dechun Agreement, agreeing to remove all its troops from the Manchukuo border. The China Garrison Army created a new puppet state in Inner Mongolia, named Mengjiang or Mongolland, in 1936. Fighting then broke out between Chinese and Japanese forces across the region.

However, Japan was able to control much of northern China by occupying it or using puppet states. By 1936, Japan could move troops anywhere in the region.

■ Second United Front

Chiang Kai-shek's policy of opposing the CCP instead of Japan was highly unpopular in China. In December 1936, the former Manchurian warlord Zhang Xueliang arrested Chiang in the Chinese city of Xian. Zhang pressured Chiang to negotiate with the CCP to create a united anti-Japan front. Negotiations resulted in a new alliance between the Kuomintang (KMT) and CCP called the Second United Front. Japan saw the Second United Front as a likely opponent to its conquests in the region.

■ China resists: the Marco Polo Bridge Incident 1937

Chinese and Japanese troops fought a brief battle at the Marco Polo Bridge near Beijing in July 1937. After Chiang Kai-shek's government refused to apologize for the incident, widespread fighting between China and Japan began throughout northern China. Japan quickly occupied Beijing, forcing Chiang's troops south. Chiang retaliated by bombing a Japanese area of Shanghai on 13 August 1937. The two countries were at war.

EXAMINING ORIGIN OF A SOURCE

- Question 10 of Paper 1 requires students to evaluate the value and limitations of a source based on its origin, purpose and content. The question is worth 4 marks.
- The origin of a source comes from several components: author, title, date of origin, type of source, and, if applicable, title, publisher and type of publication.
- Information about origin can be found in the description of a source that precedes the source's text.
- The following questions are designed to make connections between the components of a source's origin and how they affect value or limitation.

Refer to Source E to answer the questions. Use the topic: for a historian studying Japan's expansion and the international response from 1919 to 1941.

SOURCE E

Excerpt from *Modern Japan: A History in Documents* by James L. Huffman, published by Oxford University Press, New York, USA, 2004, pp. 143–4. This is a section of a speech by Japan's Prime Minister Kanoe to the Diet regarding the Marco Polo Bridge Incident. Huffman is professor emeritus for east Asian history at Wittenberg University in the USA, authoring many works on modern Japanese history.

Since the outbreak of the affair in North China on July 7th, the fundamental policy of the Japanese Government toward China has been simply and purely to seek the reconsideration of the Chinese Government and the abandonment of its erroneous anti-Japanese policies …

The Chinese, however, not only fail to understand the true motives of the Government, but have increasingly aroused a spirit of contempt and have offered resistance toward Japan, taking advantage of the patience of our Government. Thus, by the outburst of uncontrolled national sentiment, the situation has fast been aggravated, spreading in scope to Central and South China. And now, our Government, which has been patient to the utmost, has acknowledged the impossibility of settling the incident passively and locally, and has been forced to deal a firm and decisive blow against the Chinese Government in an active and comprehensive manner.

8 Who is the author of the excerpt?

9 What is the purpose of the speech?

10 How does Prime Minister Kanoe's purpose affect the portrayal of China and Japan?

CONNECTING ORIGIN TO VALUE AND LIMITATION

With reference to Source E and your answers to questions 8–10, connect the origin of Source E to its value and limitation for a historian studying Japan's expansion and the international response from 1919 to 1941.

Use the table to record your thoughts. In the first column, record key information about the source. In Value, connect the key information to how it is valuable to a historian. In Limitations, connect the key information to how it has limitations for a historian.

	Key information	Value	Limitations
Type of source			
Date created			
Perspective issues			
Purpose			
Content			

■ Second Sino-Japanese War 1937–45

Japan gave priority to the capture of Shanghai. Shanghai was China's economic centre and largest city. To accomplish this goal, Japan formed the Shanghai Expeditionary Army on 15 August 1937. China continued to attack Japanese forces in Shanghai's **International Settlement**. Japan decided to bomb Nanjing, China's capital, by air, as well as other Chinese cities. On 23 August, the Shanghai Expeditionary Army began arriving while Japanese armies in the north began moving south. Japan was ready to take the offensive.

■ Shanghai

China and Japan engaged in a large battle for Shanghai. Japan's better trained and equipped troops, as well as its superior air and naval forces, forced the Chinese to evacuate Shanghai, which was mostly destroyed, in October 1937.

■ Nanjing

Chiang Kai-shek had ordered his troops from Shanghai to protect the route to Nanjing. However, Japan formed the Central China Army in November and quickly overpowered Chinese forces. Chiang was forced to relocate China's government from Nanjing to Wuhan on 16 November. Japanese forces laid siege to Nanjing beginning on 9 December. On 13 December, Japan captured the city.

■ The Nanjing Massacre

The head of the Central China Army was Prince Asaka, Emperor Hirohito's nephew, who was an ultranationalist. Asaka ordered the execution of all Chinese prisoners. From Shanghai to Nanjing Japanese troops killed prisoners, looted property, and raped women and children.

With the fall of Nanjing, the rate of killing and raping increased dramatically. Captured Chinese soldiers and civilians, including women and children, were tortured, killed and mutilated. Tens of thousands of women were raped and then murdered. Japanese troops reportedly held contests of who could kill fastest. Some historians estimate as many as 300,000 people were killed in what came to be known as the Nanjing Massacre.

World opinion turned against Japan as a result of the massacre.

■ Further Japanese conquests

With the fall of Nanjing, Japan's army focused on gaining control of China's railways, cities and ports. The goal was to deny Chinese troops supplies, resulting in their defeat. By mid-1939, Japan:

● had captured the temporary capital of Wuhan and most of eastern China
● dominated most of China's population and industry
● had failed to bomb the new Chinese government, far to the east in Chongqing, into submission
● controlled a newly established Chinese government that managed Japanese-occupied China.

The Soviet Union provided much of China's military supplies. The Chinese army changed its wartime strategy. Japanese efforts to cut supplies to Chiang Kai-shek's government at Chongqing caused conflict with the USA.

■ The impact of the war on Japan

Japan was not prepared for a long conflict as the military believed the war would be over in three months. The military disagreed about its mission priority: the Soviet Union's threat to industrial Manchukuo or the subjugation of China. The needs of the millions of Japanese troops in China had a great impact on Japan's economics and politics. Japan's military influenced economic policy, controlled the government and banned all political parties.

EVALUATE A SOURCE USING ORIGIN, PURPOSE, CONTENT, VALUE, LIMITATIONS

- Question 10 of Paper 1 requires students to evaluate the value and limitations of a source based on its origin, purpose and content. The question is worth 4 marks.

With reference to its origin, purpose and content, evaluate the value and limitations of Source F, below, for a historian studying Japan's expansion and the international response on Japan's road to war.

SOURCE F

Excerpt from *The Struggle for North China* by George E. Taylor, published by the Institute of Pacific Relations, New York, USA, 1940, pp. 78–9. Taylor was a professor of oriental studies at the University of Washington, USA.

The Japanese really had no plan for conducting a war and pacifying the country at the same time. Third-rate political generals with no more background than that of a military college were trying to meet first-rate political problems. They were divided and bewildered. A complete collapse of oppositions was what they expected: in this they were disappointed … Conquest was rapid but incomplete …

The Japanese have no political weapons to aid them. Not for them a political *coup d'état*, a well drilled party, and be-flagged streets to welcome the deliverer. Rather a puppet government of unreliable old men without popular support, and the task of subduing the resistance of the peasantry in every northern province.

Connecting information to evaluate sources	
Topic or question addressed	**For a historian studying Japan's expansion and the international response on Japan's road to war**
Origin (title, date, author, type of source)	
Purpose (why was the source created)	
Content (use main points or ideas in content section)	
Value (how does the source help a historian understand their topic or research question?)	
• How does ORIGIN affect Value?	
• How does PURPOSE affect Value?	
• How does CONTENT affect Value?	
Limitation (how does the source not help a historian understand their topic or research question?)	
• How does ORIGIN affect Limitation?	
• How does PURPOSE affect Limitation?	
• How does CONTENT affect Limitation?	

SPOT THE MISTAKE

Below is an answer to the question. The question is worth a total of 4 marks. It requires value and limitation be evaluated, not simply listed.

With reference to its origin, purpose and content, evaluate the value and limitations of Source F, above, for a historian studying Japan's expansion and the international response on Japan's road to war.

> The source was written by George E. Taylor, a professor of oriental studies at the University of Washington in the USA. The purpose was to give an academic evaluation of Japan's actions in China. The source has value because it is a primary source. Because Taylor is an American, his biases cause limitations.

11 Read the answer and explain why 4 marks cannot be awarded.

■ Responses to the Second Sino-Japanese War

Most countries did not want to get involved in the war in China. Their concerns focused mostly on economic matters and the impact on regional colonies.

■ Response: League of Nations

China appealed to the League of Nations on 13 September 1937. The League of Nations and its members were more concerned with tensions in European affairs and anti-communist beliefs (except the Soviet Union).

The League referred the matter to the signatories of the Nine-Power Treaty (see page 16), whose declarations were ignored. The League of Nations remained uninterested and uninvolved in China.

■ Response: Soviet Union

The Soviet Union was mostly pleased with affairs in Manchuria and China. Chiang Kai-shek ended his battle with the CCP in 1936. Spending military and economic resources in fighting China reduced the likelihood of Japan attacking the Soviet Union.

The Soviets twice provoked military conflicts against Japan. Both times the Soviets defeated the Japanese, who ceded territory to the Soviet Union along the Soviet–Manchukuo border.

■ Response: USA

Preserving the Open Door Policy was the major concern of the USA. However, it did not want to antagonize Japan into preventing American trade in Asia or moving against the Philippines, a US colony. The USA prohibited shipping war supplies to China and Japan, which Japan did not need, but China did. The USA continued to export oil and metals to Japan until 1940.

In February 1938, the USA lent $25 million to China, but that was its last action in the region until 1940.

■ Response: Germany

Germany supported Chiang's anti-communist government. It also was allied to Japan in the Anti-Comintern Pact, an agreement signed in 1936 to fight efforts to spread communism by the Communist International. In late 1938, Japanese pressure ended Germany's support of Chiang.

When Germany signed the **Nazi–Soviet Pact**, it violated the Anti-Comintern Pact, causing the government in Japan to fall. The new government worked to improve relations with the Soviet Union, Germany and Italy. The **Tripartite Pact** created a formal alliance between Germany, Japan and Italy. In April 1941, Japan signed a neutrality agreement with the Soviet Union.

■ Response: China

Chiang developed a new strategy to fight the Japanese: force them to commit more and more resources until they were too exhausted to defeat Chinese forces instead of defeating them in battle.

Chiang, however, prioritized consolidating his power over China instead of fighting the Japanese and remained in Chongqing. Corruption dominated his government. In June 1938, to stop a Japanese advance, Chiang ordered the destruction of dykes on the Yangtze River, causing a flood that killed almost 1 million Chinese people.

The CCP used Chiang's actions and corruption to portray him as concerned only with his own power and wealth, not the security of China and its people.

■ Collapse of the Second United Front

Despite their alliance in the Second Unit Front, CCP and KMT forces sometimes fought one another. In 1941, KMT forces destroyed the CCP's New Fourth Army, leading to the official end of the Second United Front.

COMPARING SOURCES

- Question 11 of Paper 1 requires students to compare and contrast two sources. The comparing and contrasting of the sources should focus on the content of the sources. The question is worth 4 marks.
- When comparing sources, students should identify and explain similar content found in the sources.
- Three similarities are needed to achieve full marks for the comparing portion of this question.

For this activity, use Sources G and H to complete the table below.

	Source G	Source H	Explanation
Similarity 1			
Similarity 2			
Similarity 3			

SOURCE G

Excerpt from *The Wars for Asia, 1911–1949* by S.C.M. Paine, published by Cambridge University Press, UK, 2012, p. 103. Paine is a professor of strategy and policy at the US Naval War College, USA.

The Russians [Soviets] brokered the settlement that saved Chiang's life and created the Second United Front so that Chinese not Russian [*sic*] soldiers would die fighting Japan … Chiang agreed to join the armed resistance against Japan, free his political prisoners, end the encirclement campaigns against the communists, include all anti-Japanese parties both at home and abroad in the united front, and formulate a strategy to expel Japan from China …

The Russian strategy worked like a charm when the Japanese reacted viscerally with a full-scale invasion of China. By joining the Second United Front, the Nationalists acquired guilt by association. The Japanese saw spreading communism in China, their perennial nightmare, and were determined to stop it with their usual military solution of escalation.

SOURCE H

Excerpt from *Japan Among the Great Powers: A Survey of Her International Relations* by Seiji Hishida, published by Longman, Green & Co., New York, USA, 1939, p. 349. Seiji Hishida was a Japanese historian who received his doctorate from Columbia University in the USA, but lived and worked in Japan.

At its Seventh Congress held in the summer of 1935 at Moscow, the Comintern [Communist International] decided on a policy of organizing a united front with the Second International to oppose fascism and imperialism. At the same time, the Comintern made it clear that its future objectives were to be Japan, Germany and Poland, and that further support would be given to the Chinese communist armies fighting Japan … In Manchukuo [*sic*] the Comintern surreptitiously endeavoured through the Manchurian district committee of the Chinese Communist Party to organize cells, to win over and instigate bandits, and to direct raids by partisan [communist guerrilla] troops …

… The fundamental object of this agreement [the Anti-Comintern Pact with Germany] was common defence against the destructive operations of the Comintern.

CONTRASTING SOURCES

- Question 11 of Paper 1 requires students to compare and contrast two sources. The question is worth 6 marks.
- The comparing and contrasting of the sources should focus on the content of the sources. When contrasting source, students should identify and explain difference in content found in the sources.
- Three similarities and three differences are needed to achieve full marks for the comparing portion of this question.
- You should spend about fifteen minutes answering this question.

For this activity, use Sources G and H above to complete the table below.

	Source G	Source H	Explanation
Difference 1			
Difference 2			
Difference 3			

The route to Pearl Harbor

Ultranationalists in Japan's army and government wanted to expand Japan's empire in the Pacific. Japan's expansion provoked the USA and led to the start of the Second World War in the Pacific and Asia.

■ French Indochina

Chinese forces received most of their military supplies through a route from French Indochina. After France was defeated by Germany in 1940, Japan received permission from the new **Vichy Government** to occupy northern regions of the French colonies. Japanese troops landed there beginning in September 1940.

The USA prohibited the sale of scrap iron and steel to Japan. This hurt Japan because the USA was a major source of metal for Japan. The USA also increased financial assistance to China.

When Japan occupied all of French Indochina in July 1941, the USA acted swiftly again by:

- freezing all Japanese assets in the USA and its territories
- placing an embargo on the sale of oil to Japan
- granting China $240 million for military purchases.

Britain and the exiled government of the Netherlands also froze all Japanese assets.

■ The oil embargo 1941

The oil embargo was the most crucial development increasing tensions between Japan and the USA. The USA was the largest supplier of oil to Japan, which needed the oil for its war production and machinery. Japan had only eighteen months of oil reserves before it would be unable to continue its war with China. The Netherlands' Dutch East Indies (Indonesia) held the largest supply of oil in the region. Japan prepared to seize the colony. It was aware that such an action would provoke the USA.

■ Japanese planning

Admiral Yamamoto planned the attack on the US naval base at Pearl Harbor. The plan to destroy the US Pacific Fleet was based on several factors:

- The elimination of the fleet would hopefully cause the US government to decide not to fight Japan.
- If the USA did decide to fight, it would take considerable time to recover, allowing Japan to establish control of oil reserves in the Dutch East Indies, as well as in other territories with key natural resources.
- The USA supported the Soviet Union in its war against Germany. Japan wanted the Soviet Union to be defeated, ending it as a threat to Japan's position in Asia.

■ The Hull Note

On 26 November 1941, US Secretary of State **Cordell Hull**, in the Hull Note, demanded that Japan:

- remove all troops from French Indochina and China
- end participation in the Tripartite Pact
- renounce the Republic of China, its puppet government.

Less than two weeks later, Japan attacked US and British forces throughout the Pacific Ocean region.

MIND MAP

Events centred on French Indochina greatly accelerated tensions between Japan and the USA. It is important to understand these events and the responses made by Japan and the USA. Use the information from the opposite page to add details to the mind map below.

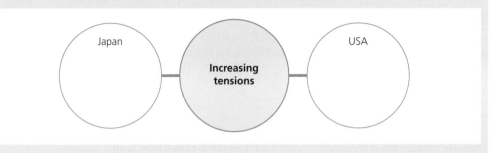

SUMMARIZING A SOURCE

- Question 12 of Paper 1 requires students to integrate knowledge from four sources and their own understanding in response to a question about a topic from one of the case studies in this prescribed subject: The move to global war. The question is worth 9 marks. It is the most valuable question and you should devote the most time to answering it.
- A successful response requires students to integrate summaries of sources.
- A good summary is based upon the main ideas of a source.
- The main idea of a source can be identified using relevant content or identifying how relevant content is connected by a bigger idea or concept.
- You should spend 30–35 minutes answering the question. It is recommended that the first five to eight minutes be used to outline your response. You should spend the last 25 minutes writing the essay.

Answer the questions below with reference to Source I. After answering the questions, write a one- to two-sentence summary of Source I.

SOURCE I

Excerpt from *From the Marco Polo Bridge to Pearl Harbor: Japan's Entry into World War II* by David J. Lu, published by Public Affairs Press, Washington, DC, USA, 1961, p. 141. Lu was a former professor of east Asian studies at Bucknell University, USA.

Prior to the outbreak of war in Europe, Japan entertained no territorial designs toward French Indo-China. Its objectives were to gain French recognition of the state of war in China and Japan's belligerent rights … Back in 1938, Japan repeatedly asked the French Indo-Chinese authorities to halt shipment of war materials to Chungking [*sic*] and had received no satisfaction. The War, Navy and Foreign Ministries [of Japan] advanced the idea of bombing the Yunnan railway which was built by French [investors], forcing a diplomatic settlement. But no concrete action was taken until the fall of 1939.

12 Why was Japan concerned about French Indochina?

13 In what way did Japan address their concerns about French Indochina to the French prior to September 1939?

14 What caused Japan to change its approach to French Indochina?

◾ Pearl Harbor and the Pacific, December 1941

Japan initiated a large-scale offensive across the Pacific Ocean region on 7 December 1941 (8 December in Asia). Its main attack came against the US Pacific Fleet anchored at Pearl Harbor in the US territory of Hawaii.

◼ The attack on Pearl Harbor

After sailing across the Pacific Ocean, the Imperial Japanese Navy (IJN) launched a large aerial assault from six aircraft carriers against the base headquarters of the US Pacific Fleet in a surprise attack.

The US navy suffered significant damage:

- four battleships were sunk; four others were damaged
- sinking or damaging of eight other ships, including three cruisers
- 188 aircraft were destroyed, including United States Army Air Force aircraft at Henderson Field
- more than 2400 were killed and another 1200 injured.

However, Japan failed to destroy:

- all three US aircraft carriers that were absent on that day
- vital oil- and torpedo-storage facilities, as well as repair facilities.

On 8 December 1941, the USA declared war on Japan.

◼ Attacks on other US territories

Japan attacked other US territories on the same day it attacked Pearl Harbor:

- the Philippines by air on 8 December (7 December in the USA) and soon afterwards a large Japanese force invaded the colony
- the island of Guam, a key communication centre for the USA in the Pacific Ocean, also followed by an invasion
- the US airbase at Wake Island, which held out for several weeks against a Japanese invasion force.

◼ Attacks on British territories

Japan also attacked British territories in December 1941:

- Japan invaded Malaya (today's Malaysia) on 8 December, as well as attacking British air and naval forces.
- Hong Kong, Britain's main colony and port in China, also was attacked on 8 December and defeated by the end of December.
- The British territory of Burma (today's Myanmar) came under threat when Japan invaded Thailand, which quickly surrendered.
- Japan and Thailand, now allied, invaded Burma soon thereafter.

Japan controlled a large area of the Pacific Ocean region. The war that began with Japan's attacks against US and British forces and territories would last until Japan surrendered on 2 September 1945.

INTEGRATING KNOWLEDGE AND SOURCES

● Question 12 of Paper 1 requires students to integrate knowledge from four sources and their own understanding in response to a question about a topic from one of the case studies in this prescribed subject: The move to global war.

● The question is worth 9 marks. It is the most valuable question and you should devote the most time to answering it.

● You should spend 30–35 minutes answering the question. It is recommended that the first five to eight minutes be used to outline your response. You should spend the last 25 minutes writing the essay.

Use Source J below and content from the opposite page to record a brief summary of the relevant content about the attack on Pearl Harbor in the table that follows.

SOURCE J

Memorandum [95] Regarding a Conversation, Between the Secretary of State, the Japanese Ambassador (Nomura), and Mr Kurusu, 7 December 1941 published by the US Department of State, Publication 1983, *Peace and War: United States Foreign Policy, 1931–1941*, published by the US Government Printing Office, Washington, DC, 1943, pp. 830–7. The Japanese Ambassador to the USA was Kichisaburō Nomura. Saburō Kurusu had been appointed a special envoy to the USA in the late stage negotiations. The US Secretary of State was Cordell Hull. The meeting took place one hour after the attack on Pearl Harbor had begun and while it was still in progress. The US Ambassador to Japan, Joseph Grew, received the official declaration of war from the Japanese government almost seven hours later at 11a.m, 8 December 1941 in Tokyo (9p.m., 7 December 1941 in Washington, DC, USA).

The Japanese Ambassador stated that he had been instructed to deliver at 1:00 p.m. the document which he handed the Secretary, but that he was sorry that he had been delayed owing to the need of more time to decode the message. The Secretary asked why he had specified one o'clock. The Ambassador replied that he did not know but that that was his instruction.

The Secretary said that anyway he was receiving the message at two o'clock.

After the Secretary had read two or three pages he asked the Ambassador whether this document was presented under instructions of the Japanese Government. The Ambassador replied that it was. The Secretary as soon as he had finished reading the document turned to the Japanese Ambassador and said,

'I must say that in all my conversations with you (the Japanese Ambassador) during the last nine months I have never uttered one word of untruth. This is borne out absolutely by the record. In all my fifty years of public service I have never seen a document that was more crowded with infamous falsehoods and distortions – infamous falsehoods and distortions on a scale so huge that I never imagined until today that any Government on this planet was capable of uttering them.'

The Ambassador and Mr. Kurusu then took their leave without making any comment.

Source	Brief summary
Source J	
The attack on Pearl Harbor	
Attacks on other US territories	
Attacks on British territories	

INTEGRATING KNOWLEDGE AND SOURCES

Using Sources A–J in Chapter 2, identify relevant content to help answer the question:

Examine Japan's expansion and the international response on Japan's road to war.

Use the table below to record a brief summary of the relevant content from each source.

Source	Brief summary	Source	Brief summary
Source A		Source F	
Source B		Source G	
Source C		Source H	
Source D		Source I	
Source E		Source J	

Source booklet

Read Sources A–D below and answer questions 9–12 in the accompanying question paper.

SOURCE A

Excerpt from the Japanese Note to the United States United States December 7, 1941, commonly referred to as the '14 Point Message,' a diplomatic note handed to US Secretary of State Cordell Hull by the Japanese Ambassador to the United States, Kichisaburō Nomura. Published by the US Department of State Bulletin, Vol. V, No. 129, 13 December 1941. This excerpt is published on the Avalon Project, Yale University, New Haven, Connecticut, USA. http://avalon.law.yale.edu/wwii/p3.asp

2. It is the immutable policy of the Japanese Government to insure the stability of East Asia and to promote world peace and thereby to enable all nations to find each its proper place in the world.

Ever since China Affair broke out owing to the failure on the part of China to comprehend Japan's true intentions, the Japanese Government has striven for the restoration of peace and it has consistently exerted its best efforts to prevent the extension of war-like disturbances. It was also to that end that in September last year Japan concluded the Tripartite Pact with Germany and Italy.

However, both the United States and Great Britain have resorted to every possible measure to assist the Chungking [Chiang Kai-shek's Nationalists government] regime so as to obstruct the establishment of a general peace between Japan and China, interfering with Japan's constructive endeavours toward the stabilization of East Asia. Exerting pressure on the Netherlands East Indies, or menacing French Indo-China, they have attempted to frustrate Japan's aspiration to the ideal of common prosperity in cooperation with these regimes. Furthermore, when Japan in accordance with its protocol with France took measures of joint defense of French Indo-China, both American and British Governments, willfully misinterpreting it as a threat … enforced the assets freezing order, thus severing economic relations with Japan. While manifesting thus an obviously hostile attitude, these countries have strengthened their military preparations perfecting an encirclement of Japan, and have brought about a situation which endangers the very existence of the Empire.

Nevertheless, to facilitate a speedy settlement, the Premier of Japan proposed, in August last, to meet the President of the United States for a discussion of important problems between the two countries covering the entire Pacific area. However, the American Government, while accepting in principle the Japanese proposal, insisted that the meeting should take place after an agreement of view had been reached on fundamental and essential questions.

SOURCE B

A political cartoon titled 'Remember' by Ding Darling, published in the *Des Moines Register*, Des Moines, Iowa, USA and syndicated nationally on 7 December 1942. Darling was a political cartoonist for more than 40 years and twice won the Pulitzer Prize, the highest award for work in journalism in the USA, for his cartoons.

SOURCE C

An excerpt of an interview given by Robert A. Fearey to the Association for Diplomatic Studies and Training in 1998. The interview was edited with the addition of an introduction by Chris Sibilla in 'The Failed Attempt to Avert War with Japan, 1941' for the *Moments for U.S. Diplomatic History* webpage on the website Association for Diplomatic Studies and Training. http://adst.org/2013/11/ the-failed-attempts-to-avert-war-with-japan-1941/ Fearey was the private secretary to the US Ambassador to Japan, Joseph Grew, during 1941 and at the time surrounding the attack on Pearl Harbor.

As the weeks passed, I became aware that [US Ambassador to Japan Joseph] Grew and [Embassy Counsellor Eugene] Doorman were heavily preoccupied with … a proposal … from Prime Minister [Fumimaro] Konoye that he and President Roosevelt meet face-to-face in Honolulu in an effort to fundamentally turn U.S.–Japan relations around before it was too late.

Grew had told Washington that Konoye was convinced that he would be able to present terms for such a settlement at such a meeting which the U.S. and its allies would be able to accept. Konoye had said that the terms had the backing of the Emperor and of Japan's highest military authorities and that senior military officers were prepared to accompany him to the meeting and put the weight of their approval behind the hoped-for agreement with the President on the mission's return to Japan …

Konoye maintained that if … [those terms were accepted] the reaction of relief and approval in Japan would be so strong that die-hard elements would be unable to prevail against it.

Grew and Doorman supported this reasoning. From the Emperor down, they told Washington, the Japanese knew that the China venture was not succeeding. Particularly after the July freezing of Japanese assets abroad and the embargo on oil and scrap shipments to Japan, the endless war in China was driving Japan into ruin. Every time a taxi went around the corner, Japan had less oil. There was solid reason to believe that the bulk of the Japanese people, except for the die-hards and fanatics, would sincerely welcome a face-saving settlement that would enable the country to pull back, on an agreed schedule, from China and Southeast Asia, even if not from Manchuria.

SOURCE D

Excerpt from *The Struggle for North China* by George E. Taylor, published by the Institute of Pacific Relations, New York, USA, 1940, pp. 78–9. Taylor was a professor of oriental studies at the University of Washington, USA.

The Japanese really had no plan for conducting a war and pacifying the country at the same time. Third-rate political generals with no more background than that of a military college were trying to meet first-rate political problems. They were divided and bewildered. A complete collapse of oppositions was what they expected: in this they were disappointed … Conquest was rapid but incomplete …

The Japanese have no political weapons to aid them. Not for them a political *coup d'état*, a well drilled party, and be-flagged streets to welcome the deliverer. Rather a puppet government of unreliable old men without popular support, and the task of subduing the resistance of the peasantry in every northern province.

Sample questions and answers

Below are sample answers. Read them and the comments around them.

9a **According to Source A, what were the reasons for Japan severing relations with the United States?**

> China failed to comprehend Japan's true intentions.
>
> Britain and the USA exerted pressure on the Netherlands East Indies.
>
> Japan's existence was endangered by Britain and the USA.

Understand what the question asks you to do, also known as the demands of the question. In this case you are asked to examine reason why Japan severed relations with the United States.

Look for key words connected to the demands of the question. Words like 'interfering with Japan' or 'frustrate Japan's aspirations' provide clues to Japan's perspective on what caused the straining of relations.

1/3. All responses accurately reflect statements from the source. However, only one of the statements relates to the severing of ties between Japan and the USA. The first response concerns the China Affair, meaning the Second Sino-Japanese War. It is part of an introductory clause that sets the background for the sentence that follows it. The second response also comes from an introductory clause that gives an example of one of the ways Britain and the USA tried to frustrate Japan's aims. Both of these responses illustrate a common mistake where students use a fragment of an excerpt without fully understanding the context in which the fragment was used in the source. It is important to carefully read with full understanding of sentences, not to look for chunks that appear to be strong evidence.

9b **What is the message conveyed in Source B?**

> Remember Pearl Harbor.
>
> The old man is mad about the death of the young man he is holding.

0/2. This response earns zero marks. The phrase 'Remember Pearl Harbor' means to preserve a memory of Pearl Harbor. However, the literal phrase does not convey a message. In this case, the memory is supposed to act as a motivator and explanation about why the USA was at war with Japan. The second response describes the illustration but not explain a message that might be associated with it. The old man is a version of 'Uncle Sam', a symbol often used to signify the USA. By examining his expression, it is possible to see his anger and determination to avenge the death of all the military men killed at Pearl Harbor. The images of the aeroplanes and soldiers inside the smoke illustrate that the entire war capabilities of the USA will be used against Japan for its attack on Pearl Harbor and that the USA will not stop until Japan has been defeated.

10 With reference to its origin, purpose and content, evaluate the value and limitations of Source C for a historian studying Japan's expansion and the international response on the road to war.

> The source is from Robert A. Fearey of the Association for Diplomatic Studies and Training who wrote an article about Japan's tensions with the USA. He wrote the source because he wanted to tell the story of problems between Japan and the USA. The source talks about how Japan might not have gone to war if some things had been different. There is some value because Fearey works for the Association for Diplomatic Studies and Training, making him an expert on diplomatic studies. The source would have been better if it had talked about more things than only Japan and the USA, because Japan did a lot of expanding before the Second World War.

Check for accuracy of statements with the information provided in the background information for sources. Inaccuracies such as the one here are easily corrected with a careful review of the source background information.

Avoid using informal language such as '[t]he source talks …]. Use more academic terms like 'states' or 'asserts'.

Use and underline the key terms origin, purpose, value and limitation. It makes claims stronger and easier for the examiner to recognize.

1/4. The response contains a number of inaccuracies. Fearey did not work for the Association for Diplomatic Studies and Training. He was the subject of an interview by the association, which published the interview in 1998 and then Chris Sibilla wrote an article that included an extended excerpt from the interview for the association's website. Fearey was in Japan during the final months before the Second World War began. He worked for the US Ambassador to Japan. His experiences make him a valuable source for this topic if his role in Japanese–American relations are noted. He was an expert on diplomatic studies, but not for the reasons stated above, which makes them valueless. The phrase '[t]he source would have been better' implies a limitation of the source. The context of a historian studying Japan's expansion and international relations would consider many aspects of Japan's expansion. Fearey's interview is valuable, but only for one aspect of the broader context.

11 Compare and contrast what Source A and Source D reveal about Japan's expansion on the road to war.

> The sources don't have much in common. They both talk about problems in China, but nothing else. Source D only looks at China, but Source A is mostly about Japan and the USA. Source D is a primary document from 1940 unlike Source A, which was written much later in 1998. Source D mentions Japan's conquest, however, Source A doesn't mention any conquests. In Source A, Japan blames the USA and Britain for its problems, but Source D does not mention those two countries at all. Source D says that Japan 'really had no plan' in China whereas in Source A they seem to have a plan for negotiations.

Do not claim that nothing is present. All compare/contrast sources will have at least two points for both compare and contrast.

The response makes a good use of a quote from Source D.

The response make effective use of conjunctions that identify differences such as 'but', 'unlike' and 'whereas'.

2/6. The response achieves 2 marks for identifying the similarity regarding Japan's problems in China and the difference regarding Japan having no plan in China, but having one to negotiate with the USA. Comments comparing or contrasting primary and secondary sources do not address the demands of a question. The question demands the student examine the source in the context of Japan's expansion on the road to war. Stating that one source is a primary source and one is a secondary source does not answer this demand. In addition, Source A is a primary source. As for conquests, Source A does not use the term conquest, but it does make reference to Japan's conquests in China and Indo-China. The task of finding three similarities was difficult with these sources. The response addressed this effectively by making four contrasting claims. It could be argued that both sources make reference to the role of Japan's military in making political decisions and that both address the surprise Japan had that resistance did not quickly end with their conquests.

12 Using these sources and your own knowledge, analyse the impact of Japanese expansion and the international response on the road to the Second World War.

Clear sentence uses the word 'effects' to show the impact of Japan's expansion.

One of the effects of Japan's foreign policy was to increase tensions with the USA. According to Source A, the USA angered Japan because it helped China, and Japan angered the USA when it attacked Pearl Harbor like in the political cartoon with the old man holding a sailor. So, the Japanese quit negotiating with the United States, which is in Source A.

Supporting sentences lack depth of understanding and effective details.

Source D points out that Japan had no plan in China. A good example of this was the Marco Polo Bridge Incident where Japan's army caused problems that the government did not want. But their soldiers there had an education from military colleges even though they had no political weapons. If China had not misunderstood why Japan went to China like in Source A, a lot of problems would have been avoided.

Many people said the Japanese were really aggressive, but they also were willing to negotiate like in Sources A and C. Maybe if those negotiations had succeeded there would not have been a war. One of the reasons Japan negotiated was because their taxis were using a lot of oil and Japan did not have a lot of it. Japan did not have a lot of resources and that is why they went to China to get resources.

Another example of using a fragment without context. Source C uses the taxi as a metaphor for Japan's oil problem.

Even though Japan was trying to bring peace to Asia as it says in Source A, their expansion had impact on the road to the Second World War. Because they made America mad, had no plan in China, and failed at negotiations, the impact was important on the road to the Second World War.

This is an example of taking an excerpt without using the context from the source. The source uses it in a context that does not explain the Marco Polo Incident, because it refers to events that happened after the incident.

3/9. The response has limited focus on the demands of the question. A few statements are appropriate, but much of the essay uses excerpts from the sources in a descriptive manner instead of an analytical manner. Using excerpts or fragments of sources as evidence without using the context in which the sources use them leads to misunderstanding and limited knowledge. The response does cite all four sources, but usually in a limited way such as the reference to Source B. The only reference to own knowledge is the statement on the Marco Polo Bridge Incident. A response to question 12 that does not make substantial use of own knowledge will be limited in the marks it can achieve. The source is effective in identifying which source is being used, with one exception; however, the style is repetitive, which can limit its effectiveness. There is no introduction. Introductions are important in setting up the rest of the response and in helping organize the essay's structure. Introductions help examiners understand the response.

Exam practice

Now it's your turn to take a mock exam.

Read Sources I–L below and answer questions 9–12 in the accompanying question paper. The sources and questions relate to Case study 1: Japanese expansion in Asia 1931–41.

SOURCE I

Excerpt from *The Wars for Asia, 1911–1949* by S.C.M. Paine, published by Cambridge University Press, UK, 2012, p. 103. Paine is a professor of strategy and policy at the US Naval War College, USA.

The Russians [Soviets] brokered the settlement that saved Chiang's life and created the Second United Front so that Chinese not Russian [*sic*] soldiers would die fighting Japan … Chiang agreed to join the armed resistance against Japan, free his many political prisoners, end the encirclement campaigns against the communists, include anti-Japanese parties both at home and abroad in the united front, and formulate a strategy to expel Japan from China …

The Russian strategy worked like a charm when the Japanese reacted viscerally with a full-scale invasion of China. By joining the Second United Front, the Nationalists acquired guilt by association. The Japanese saw spreading communism in China, their perennial nightmare, and were determined to stop it with their usual military solution of escalation.

SOURCE J

Propaganda poster titled 'Chinese Child with Soldier of the Imperial Japanese Army', produced by the Chinese Expeditionary Army, part of the Imperial Japanese Army, c.1939.

SOURCE K

Excerpt from *The Struggle for North China* by George E. Taylor, published by the Institute of Pacific Relations, New York, USA, 1940, p. 78. Taylor was a professor of oriental studies at the University of Washington, USA.

The peasantry was the only group large enough to make a social basis for Japanese rule. The method of dealing with the peasants, briefly speaking, has been one of terrorism. The Chinese people are no exception to the rule that most persons prefer peace to war, and if the Japanese could have made the conduct of war bad enough and their reprisals too severe, it is possible the peasants would not have rallied to the guerrillas. This would have been especially true where the guerrillas did not have sufficient time or leadership to train the population politically … The guerrillas came into this area in the spring of 1938 and began attacks on the railway of such seriousness that the Japanese were forced to reply immediately. The treatment of the peasantry, or such as they thought had aided the guerrillas, was very severe and most of the guerrillas were driven out.

SOURCE L

Excerpt from *Modern Japan: A History in Documents* by James L. Huffman, published by Oxford University Press, New York, USA, 2004, pp. 143–4. This is a section of a speech by Japan's Prime Minister Kanoe to the Diet regarding the Marco Polo Bridge Incident. Huffman is professor emeritus for east Asian history at Wittenberg University in the USA, authoring many works on modern Japanese history.

Since the outbreak of the affair in North China on July 7th, the fundamental policy of the Japanese Government towards China has been simply and purely to seek the reconsideration of the Chinese Government and the abandonment of its erroneous anti-Japanese policies …

The Chinese, however, not only fail to understand the true motives of the Government, but have increasingly aroused a spirit of contempt and have offered resistance towards Japan, taking advantage of the patience of our Government. Thus, by the outburst of uncontrolled national sentiment, the situation had fast been aggravated, spreading in scope to Central and South China. And now, our Government, which has been patient to the utmost, has acknowledged the impossibility of settling the incident passively and locally, and has been forced to deal a firm and decisive blow against the Chinese Government in an active and comprehensive manner.

9 a   What, according to Source I, led to Japan's military escalation in China? [3]

   b   What is the message conveyed in Source J? [2]

10 With reference to its origin, purpose and content, analyse the value and limitations of Source L for a historian studying Japan's expansion into China from 1930 to 1941. [4]

11 Compare and contrast how Source J and Source K describe Japan's actions in China. [6]

12 Using the sources and your own knowledge, explain Japan's policies towards and in China, 1931–41. [9]

Italian and German expansion 1933–40

3 Interwar conditions in Europe and Italian foreign policy 1933–6

The economic and political effects of the Great Depression

The Great Depression caused economic and social instability, as well as weakening the idea of international cooperation and the League of Nations.

Economic effects

The negative economic effects of the **Wall Street Crash** in October 1929 spread throughout the world:

- World trade declined by 70%.
- Industrialized countries experienced massive unemployment.
- Banks collapsed around the globe, including 9000 in the USA alone.

Trade barriers

Countries erected trade barriers to keep money within their own borders and to protect domestic businesses. These barriers harmed economies and reduced trade. Imperial powers turned to their colonies for economic assistance by creating systems of **imperial preference**. Some countries came to understand that colonies could ease economic problems.

The USA and the Soviet Union contained vast amounts of natural resources, leading them to concentrate on domestic concerns instead of international trade.

Political effects

Political instability developed in many countries. **Coalition** governments formed in some places. In others, alternative forms of government replaced previously stable systems. Fear of violence and communism existed in many countries.

The USA

The Great Depression led to the electoral victory of President **Franklin D. Roosevelt** and his Democratic Party in 1933. Roosevelt immediately passed laws and took executive action to address the economic problems of the USA and stimulate employment by using **deficit spending**. These actions led to massive support for Roosevelt and the Democratic Party.

Like most Americans, Roosevelt believed the USA should not become involved in foreign wars. He continued the policy of isolationism and, later, neutrality for the USA in international affairs.

Britain

After ineffective attempts to stimulate employment, a coalition government formed in 1931, known as the National Government. It succeeded in bringing some economic stability, partially by using imperial preference.

IDENTIFYING RELEVANT CONTENT

- For Paper 1, questions are numbered from 9 to 12.
- Question 9 contains two parts (9a and 9b), both of which test reading understanding of two different sources. The two parts of question 9 should take about five minutes to answer.
- Question 9a is always a narrative excerpt.
- Students are asked to identify three main points from the source. This part of the question is worth 3 marks. That means three main points must be identified. Do not go into too much detail.
- List the three main points and no more. Three sentences are enough to fulfil the demands of this question.

Read Source A and then answer the following questions that focus on identifying relevant content.

SOURCE A

Excerpt from *The Origins of the Second World War in Europe*, second edition by P.M.H. Bell, published by Pearson Education, London, UK, 1998, pp. 148–9. Bell is an honorary senior fellow in the Department of History at the University of Liverpool, UK, and has published several books.

A Foreign Office [Ministry of Foreign Affairs] memorandum put to the Cabinet in December 1931 warned that a high protective tariff along with imperial preference would separate Britain from European affairs and diminish British influence on the Continent … In 1933 and 1934 the Foreign Office urged the importance of Britain providing a market for bacon, eggs, butter and timber from the Baltic states and Poland, which might otherwise come into the economic orbit of Berlin or Moscow. Similarly, it was argued that Britain should buy cereals and other farm produce from Hungary and Yugoslavia, to prevent them becoming over-dependent on the German market. In both cases, the government refused …

1 Which phrases or key terms in the first sentence of the source indicate relevant content because they match key information found on the opposite page?

2 How does identifying these key terms help identify relevant knowledge in the first sentence?

3 What is the relevant knowledge from the sentence referenced in questions 1 and 2 above?

4 Which phrases or key terms in the second sentence of the source indicate relevant content because they match key information found on the opposite page?

5 How does identifying these key terms help identify relevant knowledge in the second sentence?

6 What is the relevant knowledge from the sentence referenced in questions 4 and 5 above?

7 Which phrases or key terms in the third sentence of the source indicate relevant content because they match key information found on the opposite page?

8 How does identifying these key terms help identify relevant knowledge in the third sentence?

9 What is the relevant knowledge from the sentence referenced in questions 7 and 8 above?

IDENTIFYING RELEVANT CONTENT FROM A TABLE

- Question 9 contains two parts (9a and 9b), both of which test reading understanding of two different sources. The two parts of question 9 should take about five minutes to answer.
- Question 9b is always a non-text source, for example, a political cartoon, propaganda poster, photograph, and so on.
- Students are asked to identify two main messages or points from the source.

Examine the following table and then answer the following questions that focus on identifying relevant content.

SOURCE B

The effects on unemployment and loss of trade of the Great Depression between 1929 and 1933. Statistics taken from *The Inter-War Crisis: 1919–1939*, second edition by R.J. Overy, published by Pearson Education, London, UK, 2007, p. 52, and *The European World: A History*, second edition by Jerome Blum *et al.*, published by Little Brown & Co., Boston, Massachusetts, USA, 1970, p. 885. Overy is a modern history professor at King's College, University of London, UK. Blum was chairman of the history department of Princeton University, USA.

Country	USA	Britain	France	Germany
Estimated unemployed workers by 1933	25%	23%	5%	26%
Decline in wholesale prices	–32%	–33%	–34%	–29%
Change in exports	–69.5%	–49.5%	–63.1%	–53.7%
Change in industrial production	–36.0%	–3.8%	–19.5%	–34.0%

10 What was the effect of the decline in wholesale prices?

11 Which row or rows are affected by changes in wholesale prices?

12 What was the effect of decreased exports?

13 Why did Britain's industrial production decrease less than that of the USA, France or Germany?

■ International impact of British economic policies

Historian P.M.H. Bell argued that Britain's trade barriers contributed to closer economic ties between central and eastern European countries and Germany. Germany became economically and politically closer to these countries.

■ Effect on military programmes

The political effects of governing with a coalition and economic concerns decreased the ability and will to build Britain's military:

- The Labour Party believed military build-up increased the likelihood of war.
- Economic pressures restricted funds to invest in military programmes.

Instead, the National Government acted to limit armaments in the early 1930s. At the same time, Italy and Germany began rebuilding their military forces.

■ France

Because France was essentially self-sufficient in food production, it did not rely on international trade like other industrialized countries. France enacted strict quotas and instituted a system of imperial preference. France did not experience massive unemployment because many citizens worked in agriculture and conscription filled its large military with young men. Politically, France suffered extensive instability.

France, like Britain, was ruled by a coalition government. Coalitions of many parties were short lived, with France having, for example, eleven governments between 1932 and 1935.

■ Germany

The Weimar government of **Chancellor Heinrich Brüning** decided to reduce government spending instead of using deficit spending to stimulate the economy. Additional economic decisions by Brüning's government harmed Germany's economy, leading to the highest unemployment rate among all industrialized nations. Germany's economy was so poor that Britain and France suspended reparation payments from the **Treaty of Versailles**.

■ National Socialism versus communism

Failures of the Weimar government permitted the rise of alternative parties in Germany.

The **National Socialists**, the Nazis, were the most popular party in Germany by 1932. In 1932, Adolf Hitler, party leader, lost a presidential election to **Paul von Hindenburg**, president since 1925. Despite the defeat, Hitler gained recognition and popularity throughout Germany.

Hitler was a nationalist, who vowed that Germany would end the humiliation of the Treaty of Versailles and regain its place on the world stage. He called for:

- eliminating dependency on other countries' trade
- *lebensraum* from former Russian land won in the First World War, but denied by the Treaty of Versailles
- land and raw materials from *lebensraum* to benefit Germany.

Hitler also preached:

- hatred for Jews and other minority groups
- that women should be wives and mothers
- that Germans were a master race destined to rule the world.

Hitler and Nazi beliefs proved more popular than communism, which:

- rejected nationalism and religion
- called for confiscation of private property
- caused the Russian Revolution and revolts in Germany after the First World War.

■ Hitler comes to power

The success of the Hitler and the Nazi Party correlated with the economic hardships of the Great Depression. From 1928 to July 1932, Nazi representation in the *Reichstag* increased from 2.6% to 37.2%. Several attempts to create a stable coalition government failed between July 1932 and January 1933. On 30 January 1933, President von Hindenburg reluctantly appointed Hitler as Chancellor.

EXAMINING ORIGIN OF A SOURCE

- Question 10 of Paper 1 requires students to evaluate the value and limitations of a source based on its origin, purpose and content. The question is worth 4 marks.
- The origin of a source comes from several components: author, title, date of origin, type of source, and, if applicable, title, publisher and type of publication.
- Information about origin can be found in the description of a source that precedes the source's text.

The following questions are designed to make connections between the components of a source's origin and how they affect value or limitation.

Refer to Source C to answer the questions. Use the topic: for a historian studying interwar conditions in Europe 1933–6.

SOURCE C

Excerpt from 'Why the German Republic Fell' by Bruno Heilig, published in *Why the German Republic Fell: And Other Studies of the Causes and Consequences of Economic Inequity*, edited by Arthur Madsen, published by The Hogarth Press, London, UK, 1941. Heilig was a journalist for newspapers in Vienna, Budapest, Prague and Berlin who was arrested in Austria in 1938 for being Jewish. He was released from a concentration camp in 1939, emigrated to Britain, and served in the British Royal Air Force during the Second World War.

Was there a link between the economic and the political collapse? Eventually, yes. For as unemployment grew, and with it poverty and the fear of poverty, so grew the influence of the Nazi Party, which was making its lavish promises to the frustrated and its violent appeal to the revenges of a populace aware of its wrongs but condemned to hear only a malignant and distorted explanation of them.

In the first year of the crisis the number of Nazi deputies to the Reichstag [parliament] rose from 8 to 107. A year later this figure was doubled. In the same time the Communists captured half of the votes of the German Social Democratic Party and the representation of the middle class practically speaking disappeared. In January 1933 Hitler was appointed *Reichskanzler* [Chancellor]; he attained power, as I said before, quite legally. All the forms of democracy were observed. It sounds paradoxical, but it was in fact absolutely logical.

14 Who is the author of Source C?

15 In what way does Heilig's profession as a journalist provide value to this source for a historian studying interwar conditions in Europe?

16 In what way does Heilig's profession as a journalist lead to limitations of this source for a historian studying interwar conditions in Europe?

IDENTIFYING SIGNIFICANT KNOWLEDGE

- Three of the questions for Paper 1 require students to identify and use significant knowledge from a source.
- Significant knowledge refers to knowledge that addresses the demands of a question. There are knowledge statements in the following table.
- Identify which knowledge statements are significant by placing a tick in the appropriate box.

17 Identify the knowledge statements from Source C above determined to be significant for a historian studying interwar conditions in Europe 1933–6.

Knowledge statement	Significant	Not significant
Was there a link between the economic and the political collapse? Eventually, yes		
For as unemployment grew, and with it poverty and the fear of poverty, so grew the influence of the Nazi Party		
The representation of the middle class practically speaking disappeared		
In January 1933, Hitler was appointed *Reichskanzler* [Chancellor]; he attained power, as I said before, quite legally		

An election in March 1933 was held to solidify Hitler's position. The Nazi Party won almost 44% of seats in the *Reichstag*. Prior to the election, Hitler had limited his opposition by:

- banning the Communist Party for burning down the *Reichstag*
- harassing and attacking opposition candidates
- restricting civil liberties.

The Nazis formed a coalition government with the Catholic Centre Party and other nationalist parties. On 24 March 1933, the **Enabling Act** was passed granting Hitler the power to create laws and sign treaties without the approval of the *Reichstag*.

The effects of the Great Depression were so traumatic that a large portion of German citizens sacrificed their representative government for promises to solve economic problems.

International diplomacy in the early 1930s

A complex system of alliances, treaties, pacts and commitment to the League of Nations created a complex diplomatic situation.

League of Nations

By 1933, the League of Nations and its commitment to collective security had been weakened.

Collective security contained a basic flaw. Governments would not commit troops to the League of Nations if their citizens objected. In addition, the two leading states in the League, Britain and France, were not strong.

France

Since the end of the First World War, France had worked to isolate Germany and enforce the terms of the Treaty of Versailles. France:

- formed an alliance with Czechoslovakia and Poland, two countries with strained relations
- sought, but failed to gain, a formal alliance with Britain as a guarantee against German aggression
- developed ties with Italy, despite Italian desires for some territory in south-east France
- maintained a large military and refused to disarm, causing tensions with Britain
- invaded the Ruhr region of Germany in 1923 to enforce reparations payments from Germany.

Political instability within France led to inconsistent foreign policy goals.

- Conservatives and nationalists, **fascists** in essence:
  - supported Italy's invasion of Abyssinia
  - opposed the Soviet Union
  - desired a strong military.

- Socialists and communists:
  - opposed a military build-up
  - desired social welfare programmes
  - supported the League of Nations and the Soviet Union.

In 1935, Germany began its remilitarization and Italy invaded Abyssinia. France was incapable of acting in response to either case because of economic and political instability.

Britain

Britain was more concerned with communism and the Soviet Union. It desired economic and diplomatic rehabilitation for Germany. Britain believed that:

- both Germany and Britain would benefit from increased trade between them
- economic recovery in Germany would hinder communism's growing popularity there
- the terms of the Treaty of Versailles needed to be revised.

However, Britain did not want to harm its relationship with France. Britain did, however, refuse to join in any alliance with France and continued to seek disarmament.

Germany

Germany's primary foreign policy goal was the revision of the Treaty of Versailles and its humiliating terms, especially Germany's territorial objections:

- Poland had been created from significant German territory.
- The region of Memel was under international administration.
- The city of Danzig was under League of Nations control and completely surrounded by Poland.
- The iron- and coal-rich Saar region was ruled by France until a vote in 1935 determined its future.

Although Germany had recognized its western borders, it felt humiliated that it could not defend itself or address concerns about its eastern territories.

IDENTIFYING RELEVANT CONTENT FROM AN ILLUSTRATION

- Question 9 contains two parts (9a and 9b), both of which test reading understanding of two different sources. The two parts of question 9 should take about five minutes to answer.
- Question 9b is always a non-text source, for example a political cartoon, propaganda poster, photograph, and so on.
- Students are asked to identify two main messages or points from the source.

Examine the following illustration from Source D and then answer the following questions that focus on identifying relevant content.

SOURCE D

A postcard published in Danzig *c.*1933–5. The illustration depicts the areas on the border of Germany and Poland (*Polen*) including the Polish Corridor and the Free City of Danzig (*Freie Stadt Danzig*). The top line at the bottom translates as 'The administrative centre of the corridor.' The line immediately below it translates as 'The network [transportation network] to eastern Germany before and after Versailles [Treaty of Versailles].' On the left side is a key showing the routes of country roads (*Landstrassen*) and railway lines (*Eisenbahnlinien*).

18 How does the illustration use symbols to convey a message?

19 How does the use of the routes for country roads and railways create a message?

CONNECTING ORIGIN, PURPOSE AND CONTENT TO VALUE AND LIMITATION

Use Source E below to identify origin, purpose and content and to connect them to value and limitation for a historian studying interwar conditions in Europe, 1933–6. Use the table to record your thoughts. In the first column, record key information about the source. In Value, connect the key information to how it is valuable to a historian. In Limitations, connect the key information to how it has limitations for a historian.

SOURCE E

Excerpt from the text of the German–Polish Agreement of 26 January 1934 published in *The British War Bluebook* located at The Avalon Project: Documents in Law, History and Diplomacy, Lillian Goldman Law Library, Yale Law School, New Haven, Connecticut, USA, published online. http://avalon.law.yale.edu/wwii/blbk01.asp

The German Government and the Polish Government consider that the time has come to introduce a new phase in the political relations between Germany and Poland by a direct understanding between State and State. They have, therefore, decided to lay down the principles for the future development of these relations in the present declaration.

The two Governments base their action on the fact that the maintenance and guarantee of a lasting peace between their countries is an essential pre-condition for the general peace of Europe …

Both Governments announce their intention to settle directly all questions of whatever sort which concern their mutual relations.

Should any disputes arise between them and agreement thereon not be reached by direct negotiation, they will in each particular case, on the basis of mutual agreement, seek a solution by other peaceful means … In no circumstances … will they proceed to the application of force for the purpose of reaching a decision in such disputes.

The guarantee of peace created by these principles will facilitate the great task of both Governments of finding a solution for problems of political, economic and social kinds, based on a just and fair adjustment of the interests of both parties.

Both Governments are convinced that the relations between their countries will in this manner develop fruitfully, and will lead to the establishment of a neighbourly relationship which will contribute to the well-being not only of both their countries, but of the other peoples of Europe as well.

	Key information	Value	Limitations
Type of source			
Date created			
Perspective issues			
Purpose			
Content			

■ Soviet Union

Joseph Stalin, leader of the Soviet Union, concentrated on domestic economic and political reorganization. The Five Year Plan begun in 1928 started the country's industrialization. Agricultural reorganization, called collectivization, was chaotic and led to famine.

The Soviet Union encouraged the growth of communist movements in the west. The Soviets also began to perceive Germany, Japan and Italy as growing threats by the mid-1930s.

Mussolini and Fascist Italy

Revised

Benito Mussolini was appointed Prime Minister of Italy in 1922, ruling the country as a dictator until 1943. He and his Fascist Party emphasized glory, empire and war. In the mid-1930s, Mussolini began efforts to achieve these.

■ Mussolini and fascism

The political philosophy of fascism originated with Mussolini and his Fascist Party. It consisted of:

- an emphasis on nationalism
- support for industrialists and (supposedly) workers
- anti-communist beliefs
- obedience to the state
- single-party government headed by an authoritarian leader.

■ Mussolini

Italy had been one of the victor nations in the First World War. It joined the Allies based on territorial promises made to Italy in the Treaty of London in 1915. Britain and France ignored these promises at the Paris Peace Conference.

The effects of the First World War became known as the 'Mutilated Victory':

- increased economic and political divisions
- unfulfilled economic and political promises
- left a huge financial debt.

Chaos, turbulence and violence spread throughout Italy. Mussolini created a gang called the Black Shirts and received support from industrialists, bankers and conservatives. His nationalism and anti-communist efforts attracted key supporters such as the King, industrial leaders and the middle class. In October 1922, he threatened to seize power from an ineffective government in a March on Rome. The King appointed Mussolini Prime Minister. Soon he was known as *Il Duce*, The Leader.

Mussolini repressed internal opponents. He:

- banned all political parties except the Fascist Party
- banned opposition newspapers
- outlawed labour unions
- used violence and intimidation.

He worked to gain support by:

- creating youth groups based on fascist ideology
- reconciling the government with the Catholic Church regarding territories seized in the nineteenth century, including Rome
- relying on propaganda to depict Mussolini's rule as a return of the glory of Ancient Rome.

■ Fascism

Fascism embraced expansion, war and imperialism. Great nations were great because they conquered and ruled other territories. The emphasis on war led to:

- women's role as mothers being stressed
- the goal of a high birth rate to supply future armies
- the belief that men should be soldiers ready to sacrifice themselves for the state.

EXAMINING A SOURCE'S PURPOSE

- Question 10 of Paper 1 requires students to evaluate the value and limitations of a source based on its origin, purpose and content. The question is worth 4 marks.
- The purpose of a source refers to why the author created the source. Knowing why a source was created can provide some insight into what kind of information was included and what kind of information may have been omitted. It also might give an indication to the perspective of the author.

Read Source F below and then answer the questions that follow.

SOURCE F

Excerpt from a speech by Benito Mussolini, quoted in *You Might Like Socialism: A Way of Life for Modern Man* by Corliss Lamont, published by Modern Age Books, New York, USA, 1939, p. 173. Lamont was a socialist, professor of history at Columbia, Harvard and other universities, and Chairman of the National Council of American-Soviet Friendship.

War is to man what maternity [giving birth] is to a woman. From a philosophical and doctrinal viewpoint, I do not believe in perpetual peace.

20 What was the purpose of Benito Mussolini giving a speech about man's nature?

21 What was the purpose of Corliss Lamont's book that contained Mussolini's speech?

22 Does Lamont's socialist ideology affect the value of using Mussolini's speech for a historian studying Italian foreign policy from 1933 to 1936?

EVALUATE A SOURCE USING ORIGIN, PURPOSE, CONTENT, VALUE, LIMITATIONS

With reference to its origin, purpose and content, evaluate the value and limitations of Source G, below, for a historian studying interwar conditions in Europe and Italian foreign policy, 1933–6. Complete the table below.

SOURCE G

Excerpt from *Italian Fascism, 1919–1945* by Philip Morgan, published by Macmillan, London, UK, 1995, p. 135.

But Mussolini's predilection was to make trouble wherever he could and disparage the forms of conventional diplomacy, using methods of internal political subversion as covert, undeclared warfare on countries he regarded as Italy's enemies. The point is not that Mussolini could be credited with a decade of good behaviour in foreign policy, but rather that the damage he could do it in the 1920s was limited because of Italy's intrinsic economic and military weakness, and the lack of counterbalance to effective Anglo-French dominance in Europe which Italy could not exploit.

Origin		Value	

• Who created the source?
• When was it created?
• What type of source is it?
  – speech, letter, diary, government document, and so on
  – primary or secondary
• Where was it published?
• Is there any important information about the author that may be useful?
  – historian, author's position, historical significance, and so on
		• What does this source let me know about the topic under study?
		• Does the source allow for a general understanding?
		• Does the source tell me only about one perspective?
		• How does knowing the origin and purpose help me determine value?	

Purpose		**Limitation**	

• Why was the source created?
• What was the author hoping to do by creating this source?
• Who is the intended audience?
• Based on the above questions:
  – is this what the author truly believes?
  – is it a partially true belief?
  – is it created for a goal(s) other than recording some truth?
		• What does this source not let me know about the topic under study?
		• If it is from a limited perspective, what does it not help me understand?
		• How does knowing the origin and purpose help me determine limitations?	

■ Fascist foreign policy 1922–34

Mussolini had to be cautious in achieving his foreign policy goals. An economy that was weak meant that Italy could not build a strong, large military. Italy's economy was dependent on foreign trade with Britain, France and the USA. Therefore, foreign policy needed to be cautious.

Italy's foreign policy relied on opportunism, especially in relation to weaker nations. Greece was forced to pay an indemnity to Italy in the Corfu Incident. A dispute between Italy and Yugoslavia over the city of Fiume, today's Rijeka, resulted in Yugoslavia giving the city to Italy. However, Mussolini's desires for territory in south-east France and the French island of Corsica were not acted on.

The idea of an Italian Empire began before Mussolini came to power. Prior to the First World War, Eritrea and Somaliland, part of today's Somalia, became colonies. With the weakening of the **Ottoman Empire**, Italy took control of Libya. All of these territories were poor, as oil had not yet been discovered in Libya, providing few benefits to Italy.

■ The Great Depression and Italy

Italy depended on the export of manufactured goods. Trade barriers erected in response to the Great Depression severely affected Italy's ability to export its goods, so Italy compensated by increasing trade with countries in eastern Europe. Italy imported raw materials and food and exported its manufactured goods.

The change in Italian trading patterns impacted Italy's foreign policy:

● Italy became less concerned with economic retaliation from Britain, France and the USA.
● Therefore, Italy had more freedom to act on its foreign policy goals.

■ Government expands control

Mussolini used the economic crisis of the Great Depression to increase government control. The government created a 'corporate state' and industrial boards involving government in business and labour concerns.

Italy relied on deficit spending to stimulate the economy. The government placed major emphasis on military spending. In addition to increasing the size of Italy's military, it allowed workers in military industries to purchase consumer goods that stimulated production in consumer industries. As a result:

● government and consumer spending increased
● employment increased
● the expansion of the army and navy provided further employment to up to 1 million men
● Italy had a healthy economy.

By the mid-1930s, Mussolini was prepared to act on his foreign policy goals:

● Italy was less dependent on trade with Britain, France and the USA.
● The government had increased control of industry and the economy.
● Italy's military was expanding both in size and in equipment.

In 1933, Mussolini reorganized the government, making himself more powerful. He appointed himself head of the ministries of war, navy and air. He also appointed himself Minister of the Interior and Minister of Foreign Affairs. In addition, he remained Prime Minister.

COMPARING AND CONTRASTING SOURCES

- Question 11 of Paper 1 requires students to compare and contrast two sources.
- The comparing and contrasting of the sources should focus on the content of the sources. When comparing sources, students should identify and explain similar content found in the sources.
- When contrasting sources, students should identify and explain differences in content found in the sources.
- The question is worth 6 marks. The recommended best approach to answer a compare and contrast question is to provide three similarities and three differences to achieve full marks for the comparing portion of this question.
- With some sources, it might be necessary to identify four similarities or differences and two similarities or differences in a response. It is never recommended to provide fewer than two examples of similarities or differences in a response.

Read Source H and Source I and identify similarities and differences. Use the table that follows the sources to organize and record your notes.

SOURCE H

Excerpt from *Italian Fascism, 1919–1945* by Philip Morgan, published by Macmillan, London, UK, 1995, p. 141.

The worst point of the Depression was 1932, when planning for an invasion [of Abyssinia] started. But the economy was beginning to recover during 1934. That recovery was certainly aided by the government's war-related commissions and contracts, which began to flow in late 1934 and early 1935, coinciding with and consequent on Mussolini's decision to invade … Preparation for war undoubtedly had an impact on employment, which by spring 1935 was down 250,000 [unemployed workers] on 1934. Some sectors benefited hugely from mobilisation, the war itself and colonial administration, obviously enough those supplying arms, clothing equipment, transportation and other logistical services for the war effort and the running of the empire.

SOURCE I

Excerpt from 'What is Fascism?' by Benito Mussolini, originally published in the *Italian Encyclopedia*, 1932, and republished in *Events that Formed the Modern World* by Frank W. Thackery and John E. Findling, published by ABC-CLIO, Santa Barbara, California, USA, 2012, pp. 11–12. Thackery and Findling are both professor emeriti of history at Indiana University Southeast, USA.

For Fascism, the growth of empire, that is to say the expansion of the nation, is an essential manifestation of vitality, and its opposite a sign of decadence. Peoples which are rising, or rising again after a period of decadence, are always imperialist; and renunciation is a sign of decay and death. Fascism is the doctrine best adapted to represent the tendencies and the aspirations of a people, like the people of Italy, who are rising again after many centuries of abasement and foreign servitude. But empire demands discipline, the coordination of all forces and a deeply felt sense of duty and sacrifice: this fact explains many aspects of the practical working of the regime, the character of many forces in the State, and the necessarily severe measures which must be taken against those who would oppose the spontaneous and inevitable movement of Italy in the twentieth century, and would oppose it by recalling the outworn ideology of the nineteenth century – repudiated wheresoever [*sic*] there has been the courage to undertake great experiments of social and political transformation; for never before has the nation stood more in need of authority, of direction and order.

	Similarities	Differences
Content knowledge		
Argument		
Perspective		

WRITING A COMPARE AND CONTRAST RESPONSE

Take the information from the table from the activity above and write a response to the question below. Review the examples of effective sentence structures given below before writing your response. A focused response will consist of six statements, one per similarity or difference. It also will completely address one demand, compare for example, before addressing the other demand, contrast.

Sample sentence structures for comparing and contrasting sources

Comparing
- Both Source H and Source I …
- Source H identifies … so does Source I with '…'
- Source I claims … similarly Source H states …

Contrasting
- Source H emphasizes … but Source I focuses on …
- While Source H asserts … . Source I claims …
- Source I examines … . On the other hand, Source H refers to …

23 Compare and contrast how Source H and Source I interpret fascism.

■ Intimidation of Germany, July 1934

In 1934, Austria's dictator, Engelbert Dollfuss, was assassinated by the Austrian Nazi Party, who wanted Austria to merge with Germany. Mussolini viewed this as a German threat to Italian interests and security because:

- Austria bordered Italy.
- Italy worked with Britain and France to isolate Germany.
- Italy worried Austria as a way for Germany to extend its influence into south-eastern Europe.
- Italy had significant economic and political interests in this region.

Mussolini announced intentions to move Italian troops to the border with Austria. Germany's army was weak and Hitler did not have full control over it. Hitler did not intervene in Austria.

More importantly for Mussolini, he had demonstrated his strength and convinced himself and others that Italy was a major military power.

■ Stresa Front, 1935

The Stresa Front was formed in 1935 by Britain, France and Italy as a united front against Germany. The Stresa Front formed partially in response to German meddling in Austria and its decision to remilitarize in 1935.

Shortly afterwards, Britain and Germany agreed to a naval treaty allowing Germany to increase the size of its navy in violation of the Treaty of Versailles. Italy and France explored the idea of military cooperation until Italy became involved in the Abyssinian Crisis.

The Abyssinian Crisis

Revised

The Abyssinian Crisis had a great effect on European relations and significant consequences for the League of Nations. It developed from Mussolini's desire for an expanded Italian empire.

■ The Italian Empire

Mussolini wanted to make Italy into a Great Power like Britain or France by creating an empire. Italy possessed colonies, but they were poor. It needed more impressive territory.

There were limited opportunities in Africa to gain colonies. Mussolini targeted Abyssinia (Ethiopia). Abyssinia bordered the colonies of Eritrea and Somaliland and the borders were weakly defended. Abyssinia offered little economic benefit and war would strain Italy's economy. But Mussolini was not interested in economics. He was interested in nationalism, expansion and glory.

■ The Wal-Wal Incident and war

In December 1934, Italian and Abyssinian troops skirmished at the small Abyssinian oasis of Wal-Wal. Two Italian and 100 Abyssinian troops were killed. This became known as the Wal-Wal Incident. Italy demanded an indemnity and an apology. Abyssinia appealed to the League of Nations. In September 1935, the League determined the Wal-Wal Incident to be minor and that neither country was at fault.

Italy, however, had been preparing for an invasion of Abyssinia since December 1934. Britain and France knew of Italy's plans, but did not want to risk their good relations.

In October 1935, Italy invaded Abyssinia. Italy's modern weaponry, including the use of aerial bombing and poison gas, quickly defeated Abyssinian troops. **Haile Selassie**, Emperor of Abyssinia, escaped to Britain. By early 1936, the fighting had ended. Italy then merged Abyssinia, Eritrea and Somaliland into one colony called Italian East Africa.

EVALUATE A SOURCE USING ORIGIN, PURPOSE, CONTENT, VALUE, LIMITATIONS

- Question 10 of Paper 1 requires students to evaluate the value and limitations of a source based on its origin, purpose and content. The question is worth 4 marks.
- The demand of the question is to evaluate the value and limitation of a source. Full marks cannot be achieved without evaluating value and limitation.
- To do this, connect value and limitation by referring to origin, purpose and/or content in the evaluation. When writing about a value or limitation be sure to add information about origin, purpose and/or content in the same sentence. Listing information about origin, purpose and content cannot attain full marks.
- It is important to use the terms origin, purpose, content, value and limitation in the response. Using these terms makes it easier to ensure that a response has fully addressed the question and makes it easier for an examiner to identify that all the demands of the question have been addressed.
- A good response should consist of six sentences. One sentence should be used for origin and one for purpose. Using two sentences for value and two sentences for limitations allows for connections to be made to origin, purpose and content at least once in those four sentences. It is important to put some content as part of these sentences.
- You should spend ten minutes answering this question.

With reference to its origin, purpose and content, evaluate the value and limitations of Source J, below, for a historian studying interwar conditions in Europe and Italian foreign policy, 1933–6.

SOURCE J

Telegrams from Mussolini to army commanders in Ethiopia, 1936, from *Mussolini Unleashed 1939–1941: Politics and Strategy in Fascist Italy's Last War* by MacGregor Knox, published by Cambridge University Press, UK, 1982, p. 4. Knox is an American professor of modern European history at the London School of Economics.

Secret – 8 June 1936. To finish off rebels, as in case at Ancober, use gas. Mussolini

Secret – 8 July 1936. I repeat my authorization to initiate and systematically conduct policy of terror and extermination against rebels and populations in complicity with them. Without the law of ten eyes for one we cannot heal this wound in good time. Mussolini

21 February 1937. Agree that male population of Goggetti over 18 years of age is to be shot and village destroyed. Mussolini

Origin	

• Who created the source?
• When was it created?
• What type of source is it?
  – speech, letter, diary, government document, and so on
  – primary or secondary
• Where was it published?
• Is there any important information about the author that may be useful?
  – historian, author's position, historical significance, and so on	

Value	
• What does this source let me know about the topic under study? • Does the source allow for a general understanding? • Does the source tell me only about one perspective? • How does knowing the origin and purpose help me determine value?	

Purpose	

• Why was the source created?
• What was the author hoping to do by creating this source?
• Who is the intended audience?
• Based on the above questions:
  – is this what the author truly believes?
  – is it a partially true belief?
  – is it created for a goal(s) other than recording some truth?	

Limitation	
• What does this source not let me know about the topic under study? • If it is from a limited perspective, what does it not help me understand? • How does knowing the origin and purpose help me determine limitations?	

◼ Responses to the Abyssinian Crisis

◼ Abyssinia

Mussolini ordered the violent repression of Abyssinia. The wholesale destruction of villages and livestock, execution of resistors and the use of poison gas demonstrated Italian ruthlessness. **Guerrilla attacks** occurred throughout Italian occupation, but with minimal impact.

◼ Response: League of Nations

The League of Nations condemned the Italian invasion of Abyssinia in October 1935 and voted to impose economic sanctions. An oil embargo on Italy would have hurt its economy. But, the League did not impose it. Britain chose not to close the **Suez Canal** to Italian shipping, claiming it could lead to war. France did not threaten Italy either. Abyssinia was condemned to defeat. In May 1936, the League of Nations allowed the Emperor Haile Selassie to speak. Italy withdrew from the League in protest.

◼ The consequences of the Abyssinian Crisis for the League of Nations

The Abyssinian Crisis revealed that the League of Nations could not enforce collective security:

- It had allowed the destruction of a member state by another member state.
- Britain and France proved more concerned with their own agendas than the success of the League.
- It had failed in Manchuria and again in Abyssinia with Japan and Italy withdrawing from the League.

The League of Nations was proven impotent and had lost all legitimacy in international affairs.

◼ Response: Britain and France

The Abyssinian Crisis created a dilemma for Britain and France. Neither country wanted to damage relations with Italy:

- In January 1935, the French Foreign Minister, **Pierre Laval**, promised Mussolini that France would not interfere in Abyssinia.
- Britain hoped to negotiate a settlement allowing Italy to administer Abyssinia without annexing it.

The brutality of the Italian invasion and occupation caused domestic political problems in Britain and France:

- Britain's National Government faced an election in November 1935 with a significant proportion of voters favouring economic sanctions against Italy.
- In France, socialists supported the League and conservatives supported Italy.

Concerns about Germany also shaped Britain's and France's actions towards Italy. Germany had a rapidly expanding economy and began rearmament.

Neither Britain nor France wanted their actions against Italy to escalate to war. Their economies were not strong enough for war and could not afford to rearm for war, especially to support a country far away in Africa. Mussolini's anti-communism was important to defend against communism's rise in Europe.

In December 1935, Laval and the British Foreign Minister, **Samuel Hoare**, devised the Hoare–Laval Plan. The plan called for giving two-thirds of Abyssinia to Italian control. One-third of Abyssinia would be an independent state with a land corridor providing access to the sea. When news of the plan was leaked to the French press, public outrage in Britain forced Hoare to resign. The Hoare–Laval Plan was abandoned.

MIND MAP

Use information from Source J on page 65 and Sources K and L below and draw your own mind map to summarize the sources.

SOURCE K

Excerpt from a speech by Benito Mussolini, 2 October 1933, regarding the invasion of Abyssinia, *Lend Me Your Ears: Great Speeches in History* by William Safire, published by W.W. Norton & Co., New York, USA, 2004, pp. 134–5. Safire wrote speeches for several US presidents and was a political columnist for the *New York Times* in the USA, a newspaper with one of the largest circulations in the world.

It is not only an army marching towards its goal, but it is forty-four million Italians marching in unity behind this army. Because the blackest of injustices is being attempted against them, that of taking from them their place in the sun. When in 1915, Italy threw in her fate with that of the Allies, how many cries of admiration, how many promises were heard? But after the common victory, which cost Italy six hundred thousand dead, four hundred thousand lost, one million wounded, when peace was being discussed round the table only the crumbs of rich colonial booty were left for us to pick up. For thirteen years we have been patient while the circle tightened around us at the hands of those who wish to suffocate us.

SOURCE L

Benito Mussolini, quoted in *Social Darwinism in European and American Thought, 1860–1945: Nature as Model and Nature as Threat* by Mike Hawkins, published by Cambridge University Press, UK, 1997, p. 285. Hawkins is a sociology professor at Kingston University, UK.

… societies are formed, gain strength, and move forwards through conflict; the healthiest and most vital of them assert themselves against the weakest and less well adapted through conflict; the natural evolution of nations and races takes place through conflict …

SUMMARIZING A SOURCE

- Question 12 of Paper 1 requires students to integrate knowledge from four sources and their own understanding in response to a question about a topic from one of the case studies in The move to global war.
- A successful response requires students to integrate summaries of sources. A good summary is based on the main ideas of a source.
- The main idea of a source can be identified using relevant content or identifying how relevant content is connected by a bigger idea or concept.
- The question is worth 9 marks. It is the most valuable question and you should devote the most time to answering it.
- You should spend 30–35 minutes answering the question. It is recommended that the first five to eight minutes be used to outline your response. You should spend the last 25 minutes writing the essay.

Read Source M below and then answer the questions that follow. Limit your answer to one sentence in length.

SOURCE M

Excerpt from *The League of Nations: Its Life and Times, 1920–1946* by F.S. Northedge, published by Holmes & Meier, New York, USA, 1986, p. 243. Northedge was a professor of international relations at the London School of Economics, UK, writing numerous books on the subject as well.

The fact is that the British and French Governments never had any intention of using force against Italy to stop its advance in Abyssinia, or even of closing the Suez Canal, which would have locked Italian forces in East Africa in a trap. Nor had any other country, though all were ready to cheer Britain and France from the side-lines, had they gone into action. Laval even regarded an oil embargo as a form of military sanction since he considered that it would have military consequences, and he opposed it for that reason. It was equally evident that, for his part, Mussolini did not intend to be prevented from conquering his victim by anything short of superior force. The conquest of Abyssinia was too important in his foreign policy; he had invested too much money, too much of his own political future, in it … In these circumstances, what course remained for the chief League Powers except to try to reach a compromise settlement which might at least keep some part of Abyssinia outside the new Roman Empire [Mussolini's Italy]? The brutality and cynicism, the blatant deception, of the Hoare–Laval proposals might be deplored, but their logic was less easily condemned.

24 What was Britain's and France's general attitude about responding to Italy's invasion of Abyssinia?

25 What was the attitude of other countries about responding to Italy's invasion of Abyssinia?

26 How would Mussolini probably have responded to forceful international intervention in Abyssinia?

27 Why did the international community not resort to using force against Italy in Abyssinia?

■ Response: USA

The USA unsuccessfully encouraged Mussolini not to invade Abyssinia. After Italy's invasion of Abyssinia, the USA banned sales of military goods to Italy and Abyssinia in compliance with its **Neutrality Acts**. The ban hurt only Abyssinia because Italy produced its only military goods. The USA refused to recognize the new colony of Italian East Africa, abiding by the Stimson Doctrine earlier invoked against Japan.

■ Response: Soviet Union

The Soviet Union proclaimed that Abyssinian independence must be guaranteed by the League of Nations. The Soviet representative condemned Italy's actions. In response to the League's failure to protect Abyssinia, the Soviet Union joined in economic sanctions and imposed an embargo on all trade on Italy.

■ Response: Italy

Italy withdrew from the League of Nations in May 1936. It was affected in other ways as well. Italy's economy:

- became more isolated from western Europe and the USA
- strengthened ties to central and eastern European countries
- focused on rearmament.

The political and economic consequences of the Abyssinian Crisis allowed Italy more independence in its foreign policy. Italy began developing closer relations with Germany.

- The **Rome–Berlin Axis** created formal mutual foreign policies and spheres of interest between Italy and Germany.
- Italy ended cooperation with Britain and France, resulting in a collapse of the Stresa Front.
- Italy declared that it would not oppose German annexation of Austria.

By the late 1930s, Germany's economic growth and military expansion made it the senior partner. Germany would shape the mutual foreign policies.

MIND MAP: INTEGRATING SOURCE KNOWLEDGE AND OWN KNOWLEDGE

Use information from Source M on page 67 and information from the opposite page to add details to the mind map.

Source M

Response:
Britain and France

Response:
USA

Abyssinian Crisis

Response:
Soviet Union

Response:
Italy

Italy 1939

Italy and Mussolini supported the conservative Spanish nationalist General Franco in the Spanish Civil War from 1936 to 1939. Italy's involvement required a large military commitment that the economy could not easily afford. Mussolini hoped that France would become involved, allowing Italy to seize Corsica and territory in south-east France. When France stayed out of the war, Mussolini decided to seize territory elsewhere.

■ Italy's interest in Albania

Albania was a relatively new country, formed as a result of the Balkan Wars in 1912 and 1913. During the First World War, Italy seized Albania as a way to supply the Kingdom of Serbia. Austro-Hungarian forces quickly drove the Italians out of Albania.

Following the war, tensions between Italy and Greece increased over Albania's borders, and included the Corfu Incident. Italy essentially established a protectorate over Albania. Albanian President Zogu signed an alliance with Italy in 1926. He established a monarchy in 1928, becoming King Zog I, thus replacing a **republic** with a **monarchy**.

■ Italy's growing control and war 1931–9

Tensions developed between Italy and Albania, beginning in 1931:

- Mussolini attempted to gain control of Albania's economy and demanded land for Italian settlement.
- Italian military advisors and instructors were forced out of Albania.
- Albania closed Italian-operated schools.
- Mussolini suspended loans to Albania.

Albania appealed to France for help. France demanded even more territory than Italy. King Zog reopened negotiations with Italy. Instead, in June 1934, Italian troops landed in Durrës, Albania's major port:

- Albania was prohibited from alliances except with Italy.
- Restrictions on trade with Italy ended.
- Italy's navy was allowed to use Durrës as a naval base.

In 1939, Mussolini sent an ultimatum to Albania demanding almost complete control of Albania. King Zog offered to give Italy some concessions.

On 7 April 1939, Italian soldiers, ships and aircraft landed at Durrës. By 10 April, all of the country was occupied. Italy annexed Albania and declared Italy's king to be the new King of Albania.

■ Responses to Italy annexing Albania

- The League of Nations refused to act.
- Britain and France did not act.
- Neighbouring countries did nothing.
- The Soviet Union verbally protested; it was the only country to protest.

■ Second World War begins 1939

In May 1939, Italy and Germany formed the **Pact of Steel**. The two countries agreed to support each other in case of war and to economic and military cooperation.

Germany promised Italy war was not imminent. Italy was reassured by the promise. Its economy was weakened by its military adventures and the use of deficit spending.

Germany did not abide by the terms of the Pact of Steel or its promise. Germany did not warn about the possibility of war with Poland until August 1939.

Mussolini declared that Italy was not ready for war. He made economic and military demands on Germany if Italy was to be prepared for war. Germany agreed that Italy could remain in the alliance without fighting in return for diplomatic and political support, and Mussolini quickly agreed.

SUMMARIZING A SOURCE

- Question 12 of Paper 1 requires students to integrate knowledge from four sources and their own understanding in response to a question about a topic from one of the case studies in The move to global war.
- A successful response requires students to integrate summaries of sources. A good summary is based on the main ideas of a source.
- The main idea of a source can be identified using relevant content or identifying how relevant content is connected by a bigger idea or concept.
- The question is worth 9 marks. It is the most valuable question and you should devote the most time to answering it.
- You should spend 30–35 minutes answering the question. It is recommended that the first five to eight minutes be used to outline your response. You should spend the last 25 minutes writing the essay.

Read Source N below and then answer the question that follows.

SOURCE N

Excerpt from *Italian Fascism, 1919–1945* by Philip Morgan, published by Macmillan, London, UK, 1995, p. 170.

The news of German plans for immediate war put Mussolini in a corner. He was bound by the alliance to join Hitler in a war he had not anticipated would happen so soon, and which he knew Italy could not really fight. It was not only a matter of Italy's military and economic un-readiness to sustain a long war. Mussolini and [Foreign Minister] Ciano paraded this in front of the Germans, in order to get them to delay things or at least accept that the alliance could not be activated then. The other reason or pretext for prevarication was the need for more time to make the Axis popular in Italy and prepare the nation politically and psychologically for war.

28 In one sentence, summarize Source N.

INTEGRATING KNOWLEDGE AND SOURCES

Using Sources A–N found in Chapter 3, identify relevant content to help answer the following question:

Examine interwar conditions in Europe and Italian foreign policy 1933–6 on the road to war.

Use the table below to record a brief summary of the relevant content from each source.

Source	Brief summary
Source A	
Source B	
Source C	
Source D	
Source E	
Source F	
Source G	
Source H	
Source I	
Source J	
Source K	
Source L	
Source M	
Source N	

Source booklet

Read Sources A–D below and answer questions 9–12 in the accompanying question paper.

SOURCE A

Excerpt from 'The Doctrine of Fascism' by Benito Mussolini, originally published in the *Italian Encyclopedia*, 1932 and later published online by the World Future Fund, a non-profit organization examining contemporary issues to develop greater commitment to investment in the future. One area of their research comprises the Global Totalitarianism Research Project. http://www.worldfuturefund.org/wffmaster/reading/germany/mussolini.htm

Fascism does not, generally speaking, believe in the possibility or utility of perpetual peace. It therefore discards pacifism as a cloak for cowardly supine [lying down] renunciation in contradistinction to self-sacrifice. War alone keys up all human energies to their maximum tension and sets the seal of nobility on those peoples who have the courage to face it … Equally foreign to the spirit of Fascism, even if accepted as useful in meeting special political situations – are all internationalistic or League superstructures which, as history shows, crumble to the ground whenever the heart of nations is deeply stirred by sentimental, idealistic or practical considerations. Fascism carries this anti-pacifistic attitude into the life of the individual. 'I don't care a damn' … – the proud motto of the fighting squads scrawled by a wounded man on his bandages … is not merely political: it is evidence of a fighting spirit which accepts all risks. It signifies new style of Italian life. The Fascist accepts and loves life; he rejects and despises suicide as cowardly. Life as he understands it means duty, elevation, conquest; life must be lofty and full, it must be lived for oneself but above all for others, both near bye and far off, present and future.

SOURCE B

A political cartoon by Sir Bernard Partridge titled 'The Answer', published in *Punch* magazine, 26 April 1939. On 14 April 1939, US President Franklin D. Roosevelt wrote a letter to German Chancellor Adolf Hitler and Italian Prime Minister Benito Mussolini asking that each leader issue an assurance that Germany and Italy would not invade countries in Europe and the Middle East.

THE ANSWER

Herr Hitler. "Take this. We are ready to guarantee peace to everybody for ever—so long as they all of them do everything we like."

SOURCE C

Excerpt from *Italian Fascism, 1919–1945* by Philip Morgan, published by Macmillan, London, UK, 1995, p. 170. Morgan was a senior lecturer in contemporary European history at Hull University, UK, and the author of several books on Italian history and Benito Mussolini.

The news of German plans for immediate war put Mussolini in a corner. He was bound by the alliance to join Hitler in a war he had not anticipated would happen so soon, and which he knew Italy could not really fight. It was not only a matter of Italy's military and economic un-readiness to sustain a long war. Mussolini and [Foreign Minister] Ciano paraded this in front of the Germans, in order to get them to delay things or at least accept that the alliance could not be activated then. The other reason or pretext for prevarication was the need for more time to make the Axis popular in Italy and prepare the nation politically and psychologically for war.

SOURCE D

Excerpt from a speech by Benito Mussolini, 2 October 1933 regarding the invasion of Abyssinia, *Lend Me Your Ears: Great Speeches in History* by William Safire, published by W.W. Norton & Co., New York, USA, 2004, pp. 134–5. Safire wrote speeches for several US presidents and was a political columnist for the *New York Times* in the USA, a newspaper with one of the largest circulations in the world.

It is not only an army marching towards its goal, but it is forty-four million Italians marching in unity behind this army. Because the blackest injustices is being attempted against them, that of taking from them their place in the sun. When in 1915 Italy threw in her fate with that of the Allies, how many cries of admiration, how many promises were heard? But after the common victory, which cost Italy six hundred thousand dead, four hundred thousand lost, one million wounded, when peace was being discussed around the table only the crumbs of a rich colonial booty were left for us to pick up. For thirteen years we have been patient while the circle tightened around us at the hands of those who wish to suffocate us.

Sample questions and answers

Below are sample answers. Read them and the comments around them.

9a According to Source A, what were the main beliefs of Fascism?

> Fascism believes that war ennobles a country and seeking peace makes cowards of a country's peoples.
>
> International organizations like the League of Nations are weak when a country is willing to defy such efforts or organizations.
>
> Fascism values duty and a willingness to sacrifice oneself for the security and glory of one's country.

The main point is identified as ennobling and the response combines information from previous sentences as descriptive of the character of the nobility.

3/3. The response identifies the three major ideas of Mussolini's doctrine. It is effective at paraphrasing the key points instead of using direct quotes. It does not confuse information from the excerpt that supports Mussolini's claims.

9b What message is conveyed in Source B?

> Hitler and Mussolini intend to expand their territory and will resort to war unless other countries give them what they desire.
>
> Because Hitler is dictating to Mussolini, it suggests that Hitler is the one making decisions and that Mussolini is subordinate and will follow Hitler's decisions.

The caption gives important information that addresses the question.

2/2. The response uses the caption, along with background information, to identify one key message. It also uses the illustration showing Hitler standing and dictating to Mussolini, as if Mussolini was his secretary, to interpret another key message.

10 With reference to its origin, purpose and content, evaluate the value and limitations of Source C for a historian studying Italian foreign policy 1933–9.

> The source is a history book titled 'Italian Fascism, 1919–1945' written by the historian Philip Morgan and published in 1995, forming its <u>origin</u>. Its <u>purpose</u> was to give a historical examination of Italian Fascism for an academic audience. Morgan's expertise as a reputable Italian historian and of Mussolini provides <u>value</u> for the source. Further <u>value</u> comes from the <u>content</u> showing how Hitler's actions and Italy's commitment to the Pact of Steel limited the independence of Italian foreign policy, eventually forcing Italy to enter the Second World War. As a secondary source, Morgan was able to use hindsight in his evaluation, adding <u>value</u> to his findings. Some <u>limitation</u> derives from the scope of the book, beginning in 1919, that covers developments outside the demands of the question, which focuses on the years 1933–9. Likewise, the <u>content</u> of the source is <u>limited</u> to the very last weeks of the 1933–9 scope.

The response connects value to origin and content.

Effective use of underlining to aid both the writing and assessment of the response.

4/4. The response addresses all components of the evaluation: origin, purpose, content, value and limitations. The response underlines the key terms, making it easy for the examiner to identify that the demands have been addressed and for the student

to ensure that all demands have been addressed. Both value and limitations are connected to origin, purpose and/or content. The response does not describe content independently of value or limitations, which is a common mistake many students make. When developing value and limitation the response makes several connections instead of only one, giving the response more depth and greater understanding.

11 Compare and contrast what Source A and Source D reveal about Italian foreign policy 1933–9.

Both Source A and Source D express willingness to go to war. Source A states that war ennobles a country and rejects the idea of 'perpetual peace'. The phrase 'an army marching towards its goal', in Source D, makes reference to war because armies are used in war to achieve goals. Mussolini, in Source A, dispenses with the belief in international organizations and alliances, as does Source D when it emphasizes the broken promises the Allies gave Italy in the First World War. Source D claims that Italy's army duty is for the benefit of all Italians, who are united behind them, which is similar to the claim in Source A that 'The Fascist … understands [life] means duty, elevation, conquest; life must be lofty and full, it must be lived for oneself but above all for others.'

Source A embraces the concept that conflict should be sought not avoided, whereas in Source D, Mussolini states that Italy had not acted, but had been patient despite growing threats. Source A states a philosophy intended to shape the character of Italy and its people, but Source D is used to justify Mussolini's intention to invade Abyssinia. Source A makes specific reference to the values individuals should follow, unlike Source D, which makes no reference to such values.

Use of direct quotes can be effective.

Uses conjunctions that show similarity such as 'as does'.

Uses conjunctions that show difference such as 'unlike'.

6/6. The response identifies six points that address both similarities and differences, with three examples for each demand. By organizing the response with one paragraph for similarities and one paragraph for differences, the response has both focus and clarity of thought. Clarity is further enhanced by identifying which source is being used for every given example. The comparison paragraph makes effective use of direct quotes in several places. On the other hand, the paragraph showing contrasts gives good examples of the use of paraphrasing a source.

12 Using these sources and your own knowledge, evaluate the effectiveness of Italian foreign policy 1933–9.

The command term 'evaluate' means to '[m]ake an appraisal by weighing up the strengths and limitations' (History Guide, first examinations 2017, p. 97). This requires you to judge the effectiveness in terms of strengths and weaknesses or successes and failures.

Beginning in the early 1930s, Italian foreign policy was effective at attaining many of its goal, such as reinstituting an empire and the glorification of the military and war. However, as tensions grew that led to the Second World War, Italian foreign policy had fewer successes and less freedom to act of its own accord.

> The response immediately answers the demands of the question.

Italian foreign policy was greatly influenced by the fascist philosophy of its leader, Benito Mussolini. As Source A shows, the ideals of embracing conflict, rejecting perpetual peace, and the weaknesses of international organizations shaped many of the goals and actions of Italian foreign policy. This was first seen when Italy posed a threat to German ambitions in Austria. The idea of the 'mutilated victory' (Source D) from the broken promises of the Paris Peace Conference became a cause to restore honour by re-establishing an Italian empire, mimicking the ancient Roman Empire, leading to further success.

> Use of source labels helps ensure that all sources have been used, for both the writer and the examiner.

The first significant expansion of the Italian empire came with the invasion of Abyssinia in 1935. Mussolini's speech in 1933 (Source D) shows the justification of Italy's impending action such as the disgrace of being left with only the 'crumbs of a rich colonial booty' (Source D). The Abyssinian Crisis caused conflict with the League of Nations, but the League had little impact on Mussolini. This defiance of the League matches his philosophy from Source A as well. Italy expanded its empire with the new territory in Africa, later expanding it into Albania. The Abyssinian Crisis was a turning point for Italy. Mussolini abandoned cooperation with Britain and France and formed the Rome–Berlin Axis with Germany, another fascist country. The Axis would later become a military commitment on the Pact of Steel.

> Own knowledge and source material are integrated.

With Italy's expanded empire and Germany's growing influence in central Europe, it appeared that Germany and Italy were the dynamic powers shaping European events. The illustration in Source B reflects this new power centre, showing Hitler and Mussolini rejecting American calls for assurances of peace. This is shown in the caption where the two leaders claim there will be peace only if their demands were met.

However, the alliance with Germany brought problems for Italy. By the late 1930s, Germany had become the dominant power in the Rome–Berlin Axis. As the international community demonstrated reluctance to check Italian and German aggressions, Hitler became bolder. Germany soon was the larger military power. Increasingly Hitler caused events that impacted international affairs. In the process, Hitler came to dictate events, giving him more influence than Mussolini, as seen in the depiction of Mussolini as Hitler's secretary in Source B.

As tensions grew over German actions in the Sudetenland and Czechoslovakia, and threatened actions again Poland, Mussolini became concerned about the possibility of war. Source C shows this worry. Italy was committed to aiding Germany in the event of conflict, but Mussolini tried to restrain Hitler or, at the least, to allow Italy to delay its commitment to the Pact of Steel. Even though Mussolini had bragged about Italy's might and new empire, the country was not ready for war, especially if it involved major European powers. He succeeded in attaining a delay, but it was clear that Italy's foreign policy was now tied to Germany's foreign policy and Hitler's ambitions.

Italy's foreign policy enjoyed early success. However, the creation of the Rome–Berlin Axis and the Pact of Steel separated Italy from the western powers and tied it to Germany. Italy and Mussolini lost much of their ability to determine their foreign policy for themselves, eventually leading them into the Second World War and defeat.

> Final paragraph summarizes the argument developed in previous paragraphs.

9/9. The response makes an effective argument that addresses the demands of the question and utilizes all the sources as well as extensive own knowledge. The response begins with a thesis that provides an evaluation of Italian foreign policy. An argument is developed using source material and own knowledge to support claims made in the thesis. Each paragraph is focused on providing detailed evidence to strengthen the essay's claims. Own knowledge is used to provide depth of understanding beyond that provided by the sources alone. The response successfully integrates source material and own knowledge in a cohesive argument. It does not separate own knowledge and source material into their own sections. Finally, the response ends with a thorough summary of the thesis and argument.

Exam practice

Now it's your turn to take a mock exam.

Read Sources I–L below and answer questions 9–12 in the accompanying question paper. The sources and questions relate to Case study 2: Italian and German expansion 1933–40.

SOURCE I

Excerpt from a speech by Emperor Haile Selassie of Ethiopia to the League of Nations, 30 June 1936. *Haile Selassie I: Ethiopia's Lion of Judah* **by Peter Schwab, published by Nelson-Hall, Chicago, USA, 1979, pp. 168–70. Schwab is a professor of political science at the State University of New York, USA.**

… The Ethiopian government never expected other governments to shed their soldiers' blood to defend the Covenant when their own immediate personal interests were not at stake. Ethiopian warriors asked only for means to defend themselves. On many occasions I have asked for financial assistance for the purchase of arms. That assistance has been consistently refused me. What, then, in practice, is the meaning of Article 16 and of collective security?

… Should it happen that a strong government finds it may, with impunity, destroy weak people, then the hour strikes for that weak people to appeal to the League of Nations to give its judgment in all freedom. God and history will remember your judgment.

SOURCE J

Political cartoon with the caption 'Pah! They were uncivilized savages, without ideals' by David Low, published in the *Evening Standard*, **3 April 1936. Low was a political cartoonist for the** *Evening Standard* **from 1927 to 1950. In 1962 he was knighted for his work.**

10   Evening Standard, Friday, April 3, 1936

"PAH! THEY WERE UNCIVILIZED SAVAGES, WITHOUT IDEALS." *(Copyright in All Countries)*

SOURCE K

Excerpt from *The League of Nations: Its Life and Times, 1920–1946* **by F.S. Northedge, published by Holmes & Meier, New York, USA, 1986, p. 243. Northedge was a professor of international relations at the London School of Economics, UK, writing numerous books on the subject as well.**

The fact is that the British and French Governments never had any intention of using force against Italy to stop its advances in Abyssinia, or even of closing the Suez Canal, which would have locked Italian forces in East Africa in a trap. Nor had any other country, though all were ready to cheer Britain and France from the side-lines, had they gone into action. Laval even regarded an oil embargo as a form of military sanction since he considered that it would have military consequences, and he opposed it for that reason. It was equally evident that, for his part, Mussolini did not intend to be prevented from conquering his victim by anything short of superior force. The conquest of Abyssinia was too important in his foreign policy; he had invested too much money, too much of his own political future in it … In these circumstances, what course remained for the chief League Powers except to try to reach a compromise settlement which might at least keep some part of Abyssinia outside the new Roman Empire [Mussolini's Italy]? The brutality and cynicism, the blatant deception, of the Hoare–Laval proposals might be deplored, but their logic was less easily condemned.

SOURCE L

Excerpt from *Origins of the Second World War* by A.J.P. Taylor, published by Penguin Books, London, UK, 1991, p. 36. Taylor was a British historian who wrote many books on European history and lectured at many British universities.

The real weakness was within the League. Though the French could not afford to quarrel with Great Britain, Laval was dismayed by the crumbling of the Stresa front. The old British arguments in favour of conciliation and against the automatic working of collective security reappeared in French mouths. France applied sanctions; but Laval assured Mussolini now, if not earlier, that Italy's oil supplies would not be interfered with. There was divergence of views in Great Britain also. The division was not merely between the 'idealists' who supported the League of Nations and the cynics who believed that collective security always involved risk and burdens for Great Britain, without any compensating gain. The division was also one between the generations. Younger men, represented by Eden, were strenuously anti-Italian and were much more ready to conciliate Germany. The traditionalists, particularly strong in the foreign office, were concerned only with the German danger; they regarded the League of Nations as a nuisance and wished to win back Italy for the united front against Germany. Vansittart, permanent under-secretary at the foreign office, took this view; from first to last he was the unrepentant advocate of alliance with Italy, which he seemed to treat as the solution for every problem. Even Winston Churchill, who was already sounding the alarm over Germany, remained out of the country during the autumn of 1935 so as to avoid having to pronounce for or against Italy. On the surface British policy was firm for collective security. Behind the scenes influential figures waited to put forward some version of the compromise which Mussolini had rejected in the previous June. At that time, the Emperor of Abyssinia, too, had been obstinate – confident that a martyr's adherence to collective security would strengthen his tottering throne, as indeed it did, though in a longer run than he expected.

9 a How, according to Source I, did Haile Selassie justify his call for assistance from the League of Nations? [3]

   b What is the message conveyed in Source J? [2]

10 With reference to its origin, purpose and content, analyse the value and limitations of Source K for a historian studying Italy's invasion of Abyssinia and the resulting crisis. [4]

11 Compare and contrast how Source K and Source L explain the failures of the League of Nations in the Abyssinian Crisis. [6]

12 Using the sources and your own knowledge, analyse Italian expansion in Abyssinia and Italian foreign policy 1933–6. [9]

4 German foreign policy 1933–40

Revised ☐

Hitler and Nazi Germany 1933–8

Revised ☐

Adolf Hitler was appointed Chancellor of Germany in January 1933 and quickly established a single-party state. By 1938, he had total power. His foreign policy, based on fascist ideology, became more aggressive as he became more powerful.

■ Hitler and the consolidation of power 1933–8

Hitler and the Nazi Party implemented the policy of *Gleichschaltung*, meaning 'making the same' in German, merging the government with the party. Key effects included:

- banning all political parties except the Nazi Party
- abolishing labour unions
- filling governing organizations and offices with Nazi Party officials
- giving all police power to the *Schutzstaffel*, **SS**.

Hitler also eliminated threats to his power from members of the Nazi Party. In 1934, he executed his most serious rivals within the party.

Only the German army evaded his control, where the conservative nobility, who made up the officer corps, did not trust Hitler. By 1938, the top commanders had been replaced with men loyal to Hitler. He now controlled the army.

With each increase in power, Hitler felt more confident challenging the limitations of the Treaty of Versailles.

■ Nazi Germany's economy 1933–9

The Nazis' early economic policies focused on the problems caused by the Great Depression.

■ The 'New Plan'

In 1934, the 'New Plan,' introduced by Hjalmar Schacht, German Minister of Economics, gave more power to the government to control the economy. Germany only traded with countries if their exports were equal to or greater in value than their imports. Trade increased with states that exported raw materials to Germany and bought German manufactured goods:

- Food became cheaper in Germany.
- More money became available to use for rearmament.
- Increased trade with central and eastern European states made them rely economically, and therefore politically, on Germany.

Germany's economy recovered more quickly than other states. Because Britain and France relied on imperial preference, this allowed Germany to increase its political influence throughout the rest of Europe.

■ The Four Year Plan 1936–9

The New Plan had been designed to strengthen Germany's economy, but pressure caused increasing spending on military priorities. Schacht wanted to stay focused on the economy.

In 1936, the Four Year Plan, led by Hermann Goering, was announced. Schacht resigned as Minister of Economics in 1937. The government hoped to gain greater self-sufficiency. This would reduce Germany's vulnerability to **embargoes** and blockades like the one in the First World War. However, the main goal was to support rearmament.

The historian Richard Overy believed the Four Year Plan was designed to prepare Germany for war, probably sometime in the 1940s.

German military production increased, but it contributed to inflation. Some historians argue that political pressure from workers and economic problems were a major cause of Germany going to war in 1939.

IDENTIFYING RELEVANT CONTENT

- For Paper 1, questions are numbered from 9 to 12.
- Question 9 contains two parts (9a and 9b), both of which test reading understanding of two different sources. The two parts of question 9 should take about five minutes to answer.
- Question 9a is always a narrative excerpt. Students are asked to identify three main points from the source.

Read Source A and then answer the following questions that focus on identifying relevant content.

SOURCE A

Excerpt from *The Origin of the Second World War in Europe*, second edition by P.M.H. Bell, published by Pearson Education, London, UK, 1998, p. 158. Bell is an honorary senior fellow in the Department of History at the University of Liverpool, UK, and has published several books.

… he [Schacht] introduced his 'New Plan' for German foreign trade, based on the principles of buying nothing that could not be paid for by foreign exchange earned by German exports, and of making imports conform to national needs as decided by the government. All imports were subject to licences, which were used to differentiate between essential and non-essential items, with raw materials and food classified as essential. Whenever possible, imports were bought only from countries which were willing to accept German goods in return; and any foreign exchange involved was to be paid into a clearing account, and not used freely by the exporting country.

1   How was foreign trade conducted under the New Plan?
2   What items were most likely to be imported?

IDENTIFYING RELEVANT CONTENT FROM AN ILLUSTRATION

- Question 9 contains two parts (9a and 9b), both of which test reading understanding of two different sources. The two parts of question 9 should take about five minutes to answer.
- Question 9b is always a non-text source, for example, a political cartoon, propaganda poster, photograph, and so on. Students are asked to identify two main messages or points from the source.

Examine Source B and then answer the following questions that focus on identifying relevant content.

SOURCE B

Photomontage by John Heartfield published on the cover of the weekly magazine *Arbeiter–Illustrierte–Zeitung (AIZ)* (*The Workers Pictorial Newspaper*) on 19 December 1935. *AIZ* was a socialist newspaper with a broad range of topics. Heartfield had joined the German Communist Party in 1919 and produced over 280 covers for *AIZ*. In March 1933, Heartfield and *AIZ* fled to Prague until the paper was forced to close permanently in 1938. Heartfield escaped to England where he remained for the duration of the Second World War. The caption reads: 'Hurrah, There's No Butter Left! Goering in his Hamburg speech: "Ore has always made an empire strong, butter and lard have made a people fat at most".'

3   How does the caption help convey the illustration's message?
4   How does the issue of symbolism convey the illustration's message?

■ Rearmament

The Treaty of Versailles greatly restricted Germany's military.

■ Vulnerability after 1919

Germany was disarmed, but the countries that bordered it, France and Poland, had large armies and formed an alliance. France also formed the Little Entente with Czechoslovakia, Romania and Yugoslavia in 1920 and 1921. Many Germans felt encircled.

When France and Belgium occupied the Ruhr region to enforce reparations payments, the German sense of vulnerability increased. Growing concerns over an industrializing Soviet Union added to Germany's desire to defend itself.

■ World Disarmament Conference 1932

The League of Nations held a **World Disarmament Conference** in Geneva, Switzerland, in 1932. The goal was to decrease the size of armies.

France refused to reduce its military without a security guarantee from Britain and the USA. Both countries refused. France's insistence on a large army increased Germany's desire for rearmament. Germany left the conference and soon withdrew from the League of Nations.

■ Rearmament begins

Germany began rearmament in 1935, violating the terms of the Treaty of Versailles. Germany:

● began conscription
● established a large air force
● expanded the navy.

By 1939, Germany had a large army, air force and military arms production capability. During this time the Great Depression caused most countries to limit military spending.

■ International response to rearmament, April 1935

■ Stresa Front, April 1935

Leaders of Britain, France and Italy created the Stresa Front in response to Germany's rearmament. They condemned German violations of the Treaty of Versailles and agreed to cooperate with regard to Germany. Because of the Great Depression, none of the countries had the ability to act militarily against Germany.

Hitler gave assurances that he had no aggressive intentions.

■ France's response

Although France was a great military power, it sought a new ally. Britain and Poland were not reliable. In May 1935, France and the Soviet Union signed the Franco-Soviet Treaty of Mutual Assurance. They agreed to:

● work through the League of Nations for peace
● aid each other in case of conflict.

Political division in France prevented the agreement from becoming a full military alliance. To prevent an invasion, France built fortifications along its border with Germany, called the Maginot Line.

■ Britain's response

Following the First World War, there was little support for rearmament. Economic problems from the Great Depression strengthened this reluctance. Germany's decision to rearm changed British attitudes towards rearmament. Britain began rearmament on a large scale. Military spending increased by over 600% between 1935 and 1939.

IDENTIFYING SIGNIFICANT KNOWLEDGE

Three of the questions for Paper 1 require students to identify and use significant knowledge from a source. Significant knowledge refers to knowledge that addresses the demands of a question.

Read the question and Source C below. In the following table, there are knowledge statements. Identify which knowledge statements are significant by placing a tick in the appropriate box. The knowledge statements identified as significant could be used in identifying relevant content, in comparing and contrasting sources, and as knowledge from sources in the open-ended question of Paper 1.

SOURCE C

Excerpt from 'The Nazi Economy – Was It Geared to War?' by Richard Overy, published in *History Review*, No. 31, September 1998. *History Review* was a journal devoted to publishing authoritative articles by modern historians; it ended in 2012. Overy is a prominent historian and history professor at Exeter University, UK.

… The armed forces themselves were anxious to rebuild German military power cautiously, step-by-step, so that they could control its pace and character themselves. The first priority was to rebuild the infrastructure of military life – barracks, airfields, training schools – that had been shut down or destroyed during the period of enforced disarmament. The first air force production programmes were largely devoted to building trainer aircraft. Between 1934 and 1938 some 50 per cent of aircraft production was made of trainer aircraft and only 18 per cent of combat planes. Tank production was slow to get going and the programme for naval shipbuilding laid down in 1934 had achieved little before the late 1930s. Remilitarisation on any scale took time to achieve because Germany began in 1933 from a very low base.

5   Identify the knowledge statements determined to be significant for German expansion by placing a tick in the appropriate box.

Knowledge statement	Significant	Not significant
The armed forces themselves were anxious to rebuild German military power cautiously, step-by-step, so that they could control its pace and character themselves		
Infrastructure of military life – barracks, airfields, training schools – that had been shut down or destroyed during the period of enforced disarmament		
The first air force production programmes were largely devoted to building trainer aircraft		
Tank production was slow to get going and the programme for naval shipbuilding laid down in 1934 had achieved little before the late 1930s		
Remilitarization on any scale took time to achieve because Germany began in 1933 from a very low base		

MIND MAP: INTEGRATING SOURCE KNOWLEDGE AND OWN KNOWLEDGE

Use information from Source C above and information from the opposite page to add details to the mind map.

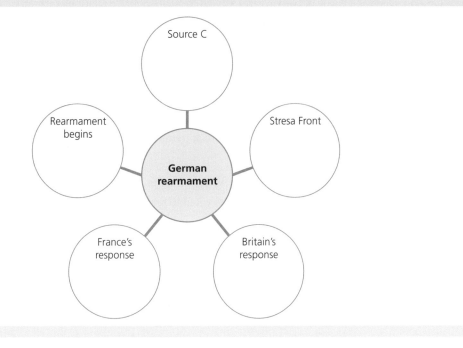

Germany's foreign policy 1933–5

Between 1933 and 1935, Hitler had a cautious foreign policy. Germany's economy and military was weak. Politically, Hitler was consolidating his power.

■ Nazism and foreign policy

Nazi philosophy and beliefs influenced German foreign policy:

- completely revising the Treaty of Versailles
- **pan-Germanism** or all Germans should live in Germany
- anti-communism
- Germany needed living space or *lebensraum*

- Germans were a superior race destined to conquer and rule non-German inferior races
- democracy created weak states
- Germany needed strong leadership.

■ The Polish–German Non-Aggression Pact, January 1934

In January 1934, Poland and Germany signed the Polish–German Non-Aggression Pact. Both countries agreed not to attack each other for a period of ten years. Poland felt it had little to fear from Germany. It:

- possessed a large army
- had an alliance with France

- worried more about the Soviet Union.

Germany benefited because it:

- could rearm without fear about Poland
- had weakened the alliance between France and Poland

- would lead to more trade with Poland, a source of food and metals.

■ International response: France

France was furious with Poland. Their alliance and trust was weakened. But, France could do little about it. The non-aggression pact may have been a cause of France seeking better relations with the Soviet Union.

■ International response: Soviet Union

Favourable relations had existed between Germany and the Soviet Union since the **Rapallo Treaty** established diplomatic relations in 1922. Trade and limited military cooperation soon developed. This cooperation continued after the Nazis came to power.

The Polish–German Non-Aggression Pact ended all cooperation. The Soviets worried about Poland concentrating military forces on their border and a potential alliance between Germany and Poland.

The Soviet Union joined the League of Nations and worked to create positive relations with other countries.

■ Austria 1934

Pan-Germanism appealed to many in Austria and Germany, including Hitler who was born in Austria. Political instability in Austria may have led to the desire for stability offered by Germany.

In June 1934, Hitler discussed with Mussolini the idea of making Austria a German **satellite state**. Mussolini rejected this idea. Hitler encouraged the Austrian Nazi Party to stage a coup (see page 64). This led to the Stresa Front. Germany was too weak to intervene militarily.

■ Saar Plebiscite 1935

The Saar was an iron- and coal-rich region in Germany administered by the League of Nations. In a January 1935 **plebiscite**, more than 90% of Saar residents voted to join Germany.

■ Anglo-German Naval Treaty, June 1935

In June 1935, Britain and Germany signed the Anglo-German Naval Treaty. Britain considered Germany had legitimate concerns, but should be limited militarily. For Britain, the treaty accomplished these goals by limiting Germany's navy to 35% of Britain's navy.

France and Italy judged the treaty as encouraging German rearmament. The Stresa Front was seriously weakened and then collapsed with Italy's invasion of Abyssinia later in 1935.

EXAMINING ORIGIN OF A SOURCE AND PURPOSE

- Question 10 of Paper 1 requires students to evaluate the value and limitations of a source based on its origin, purpose and content. This question is worth 4 marks.
- The origin of a source comes from several components: author, title, date of origin, type of source, and, if applicable, title, publisher and type of publication. Information about origin can be found in the description of a source that precedes the source's text.
- The following questions are designed to make connections between the components of a source's origin and how they affect value or limitation.

Refer to Source D to answer the questions. Use the topic: for a historian studying German foreign policy 1933–40.

SOURCE D

Excerpt from a memo from State Secretary for Foreign Affairs B.W. von Bülow to German Chancellor Hitler, August 1934, quoted in *Documents on Nazism 1919–1945* by Jeremy Noakes and Geoffrey Pridham, published by University of Exeter Press, UK, 1995, p. 662. Noakes is a professor of history at the University of Exeter, UK. Pridham is a senior research fellow in politics at the University of Bristol, UK.

In judging the situation we should never overlook the fact that no kind of rearmament in the next few years could give us military security. Even apart from our isolation, we shall for a long time yet be hopelessly inferior to France in the military sphere. A particularly dangerous period will be 1934–5 on account of the reorganization of the *Reichswehr* [German army].

6 A memo is usually used as a formal means of communication from one office to another. They are for internal communication only. In what ways does a memo give value to a historian?

7 What was von Bülow's purpose in sending the memo to Hitler?

8 To what extent does von Bülow's position provide value to a source he wrote for a historian studying German foreign policy 1933–40?

EXAMINING CONTENT OF A SOURCE

- Content refers to the information contained in a source.
- Content value comes from information in the source that matches the topic being examined.
- Content limitation comes from information in the source that does not match the topic being examined.
- Content limitation also can result from information found in the source that addresses only part of the scope of the topic being examined.

For the questions below, refer to Source E below. The following questions are designed to make connections between the content of a source and how it affects value or limitation. Use the topic: for a historian studying German foreign policy 1933–40.

SOURCE E

Excerpt of a letter from British Foreign Secretary Sir John Simon to King George V of the United Kingdom, February 1935, quoted in *Sir Gerald Fitzmaurice and the World Crisis: A Legal Advisor in the Foreign Office 1930–1945* by Anthony Carty, published by Springer, New York, USA, 2000, p. 179. Carty is a law professor at the University of Aberdeen, UK.

The practical choice is between a Germany which continues to rearm without any regulation or agreement and a Germany which, through getting a recognition of its rights and some modification of the Peace Treaties, enters into the comity [community] of nations and contributes, in this and other ways, to European stability.

9 What is Simon's view on relations with Germany?

10 How is Simon's recommendation valuable for a historian studying German foreign policy 1933–40?

11 What are the limitations of Source E?

Germany's foreign policy 1936–9

Germany's improved economy and strengthened military encouraged Hitler to pursue a more aggressive foreign policy. Hitler benefited from other developments as well:

- Britain was sympathetic to many of Germany's goals.
- France and Britain could not agree how to respond to German actions.
- Few countries would cooperate with the Soviet Union.
- Italy developed a favourable foreign policy towards Germany.

■ Remilitarization of the Rhineland, March 1936

The Treaty of Versailles created a demilitarized Rhineland, German territory bordering France, Belgium and Luxembourg. Germany's inability to defend the Rhineland was one of the sources of humiliation. Demilitarization made Germany vulnerable to attack.

Hitler saw the political turmoil from the Abyssinian Crisis as an opportunity to act in the Rhineland. In December 1935, he ordered the German army to create an occupation plan. Diplomatically, Germany argued that the Franco-Soviet Treaty of Mutual Assurance altered the **Locarno treaties**, permitting Germany to alter other agreements.

On 7 March 1936, German troops reoccupied and therefore remilitarized the Rhineland. They were few in number in order to minimize France's reaction.

■ International response: France and Britain

France did not respond.

- Germany did not violate the French border.
- The French army believed Germany would not attack through the Rhineland.
- Military plans prepared for a defensive war and therefore had no plans to invade Germany, even if the Rhineland was remilitarized.
- France refused to fight Germany alone.
- Military spending increased.

Britain:

- reassured France of support should Germany invade
- viewed the occupation as Germany walking in its 'own back garden'
- believed it removed one of Germany's grievances against France and Britain, and therefore
- hoped Germany would become more cooperative.

Revision of the Treaty of Versailles became acceptable. Germany was emerging as a major economic and military power.

■ Germany ends diplomatic isolation 1936

The Abyssinian Crisis made Italy a diplomatically isolated country like Germany. Both countries were fascist and anti-communist as well. With these commonalities, they began forging a closer relationship.

■ The Rome–Berlin Axis, October 1936

In October 1936, Germany and Italy formed the Rome–Berlin Axis, a new diplomatic relationship. It was intended to show that Germany and Italy were the new dominant powers in world affairs.

■ The Anti-Comintern Pact, November 1936

The Soviet-sponsored Communist International (Comintern) supported communist groups around the world. Japan and Germany formalized their opposition to these efforts in the Anti-Comintern Pact signed in November 1936. The agreement was primarily symbolic, but did announce that neither country was diplomatically isolated. Global anti-communist sentiment minimized concern with the new relationship. Italy joined the Pact in November 1937.

CONNECTING ORIGIN, PURPOSE AND CONTENT TO VALUE AND LIMITATION

Use Source F below to identify origin, purpose and content and to connect them to value and limitation for a historian studying German foreign policy 1933–40.

- Use the table to record your thoughts.
- In the first column, record key information about the source.
- In Value, connect the key information to how it is valuable to a historian.
- In Limitations, connect the key information to how it has limitations for a historian.

SOURCE F

Excerpt of a speech by Benito Mussolini in Milan, Italy, 1 November 1936, quoted in *The Causes of the Second World War* by Anthony Crozier, published by Blackwell Publishers, Oxford, UK, 1997, p. 121. Crozier was a history lecturer at Queen Mary College, University of London, UK.

The Berlin conversations have resulted in an understanding between our two countries over certain problems which have been acute. By these understandings … this Berlin–Rome line is … an axis around which can revolve all those European states with a will to collaboration and peace.

	Key information	Value	Limitations
Type of source			
Date created			
Perspective issues			
Purpose			
Content			

EVALUATE A SOURCE USING ORIGIN, PURPOSE, CONTENT, VALUE, LIMITATIONS

- Question 10 of Paper 1 requires students to evaluate the value and limitations of a source based on its origin, purpose and content. This question is worth 4 marks.
- The demand of the question is to evaluate the value and limitation of a source. Full marks cannot be achieved without evaluating value and limitation.
- To do this, connect value and limitation by referring to origin, purpose and/or content in the evaluation. When writing about a value or limitation be sure to add information about origin, purpose and/or content in the same sentence. Listing information about origin, purpose and content cannot attain full marks.
- It is important to use the terms origin, purpose, content, value and limitation in the response. Using these terms makes it easier to ensure that a response has fully addressed the question and makes it easier for an examiner to identify that all the demands of the question have been addressed.
- A good response should consist of six sentences. One sentence should be used for origin and one for purpose. Using two sentences for value and two sentences for limitations allows for connections to be made to origin, purpose and content at least once in those four sentences. It is important to put some content as part of these sentences.
- You should spend ten minutes answering this question.

With reference to its origin, purpose and content evaluate the value and limitations of Source J, below, for a historian studying German foreign policy 1933–40.

SOURCE G

Excerpt from *The Origins of the Second World War* by A.J.P. Taylor, Penguin Books, London, UK, 1961, pp. 129–30. First published in 1961 by Hamish Hamilton, this book has been most recently published by Penguin Books in 2001. Taylor was a British historian who wrote many books on European history and was a lecturer at many British universities.

Hitler's excuse was the French government's ratification of the Franco-Soviet pact on 27 February 1936. This, he claimed, had destroyed the assumptions of Locarno; not much of an argument, but a useful appeal no doubt to anti-Bolshevik feeling in Great Britain and France. The actual move on 7 March was a staggering example of Hitler's strong nerve. Germany had literally no forces available for war. The trained men of the old *Reichswehr* [German army] were now dispersed as instructors among the new mass army; and this new army was not yet ready. Hitler assured his protesting generals that he would withdraw his token force at the first sign of French action; but he was unshakably confident that no action would follow.

The reoccupation of the Rhineland did not take the French by surprise. They had been brooding on it apprehensively ever since the beginning of the Abyssinian affair.

■ *Anschluss*, March 1938

A factor in the formation of the Rome–Berlin Axis was Italy withdrawing objections to Germany annexing Austria. In addition to the concept of Pan-Germanism, Austria offered other key advantages to Germany:

- large industrial development
- many skilled workers
- significant gold reserves
- vital natural resources.

By 1938, Germany's economy and military were strong. Hitler began pursuing *Anschluss*, German for connection or annexation, with Austria.

The Austrian government entered negotiations with Germany to prevent annexation. Hitler demanded:

- the appointment of **Arthur Seyss-Inquart**, an Austrian Nazi Party member, as Minister of Public Security, giving him control of all police
- the release of all jailed Nazi Party members.

When the Austrian government agreed to these demands, Hitler declared that millions of suppressed Germans be reunited with Germany. This was a challenge to Austrian independence.

In an attempt to prevent a German takeover, Austria's Chancellor Kurt Schuschnigg scheduled a plebiscite to decide if Austrians wanted *Anschluss*. Hitler claimed that rioting broke out in Austria requiring Germany to send troops to restore order. He then threatened invasion unless Schuschnigg resigned, which he did. Seyss-Inquart was made Chancellor, and he immediately requested German assistance.

On 12 March 1938, German troops entered Austria. The next day Austria became part of Germany in violation of the Treaty of Versailles. A plebiscite in April resulted in over 99% of Austrians voting in favour of *Anschluss*. The League of Nations did nothing in response because:

- Austria had invited German troops to enter the country
- Austrian citizens overwhelmingly voted in favour of joining Germany.

■ International response: Britain and France

Neither Britain nor France made any serious objection to *Anschluss*:

- They could do little militarily.
- Both countries believed Germany could be useful in the fight against communism.
- It appeared to be a case of Germans wanting to live in Germany.

■ Appeasement

Appeasement was the policy of negotiating by Britain and France to address Germany's grievances with the Treaty of Versailles. Many believed it encouraged Hitler to be more aggressive because the policy made Britain and France seem weak. More recent scholarship views appeasement as much more complex. Britain believed negotiating made more sense than confrontation, especially since Britain was still rebuilding its military. Many at the time saw Germany's demands as reasonable.

■ International response: Soviet Union

The Soviet Union protested, but had no other options. Internal political strife in the form of **purges** resulted in the imprisonment and execution of many senior government and military officials, including its foreign policy and diplomatic experts. The violence contributed to Britain and France having little reason to work with the Soviet Union.

IDENTIFYING RELEVANT CONTENT FROM AN ILLUSTRATION

- Question 9 contains two parts (9a and 9b), both of which test reading understanding of two different sources. The two parts of question 9 should take about five minutes to answer.
- Question 9b is always a non-text source, for example, a political cartoon, propaganda poster, photograph, and so on. Students are asked to identify two main messages or points from the source.

Examine the following illustration from Source H and then answer the following questions that focus on identifying relevant content.

SOURCE H

Photograph of the Adolf Loos House in Vienna, 1938. The banner on the house has been put in place in preparation for the plebiscite in April 1938 to confirm reunification with German that had occurred one month earlier when German troops entered Austria. The banner reads: 'The Same blood belongs to a common empire.' The Adolf Loos House was a famous, but controversial building in Vienna, named after the famous architect who designed it.

12 What does the photograph suggest about Nazi influence in Austria prior to the plebiscite?

13 How does the wording on the banner help historians understand the *Anschluss*?

INTEGRATING SOURCE KNOWLEDGE AND OWN KNOWLEDGE

Use information from Source H above and information from the opposite page to add details about the *Anschluss* to the table below.

Source	Brief summary
Source H	
Germany	
Austria	
Britain	
France	
Appeasement	
Soviet Union	

■ Sudeten Crisis, October 1938

Inspired by the *Anschluss*, Germans living in the Sudeten area of Czechoslovakia and the **Sudeten German Party**, close allies of the Nazi Party, demanded to become part of Germany.

After meeting with Hitler in March 1938, **Konrad Henlein**, head of the Sudeten German Party, issued a list of demands called the Karlsbad Programme. The main demand was autonomy for Germans in Czechoslovakia. President Edvard Beneš of Czechoslovakia rejected autonomy and offered greater rights for Sudeten Germans. Many saw Henlein working on behalf of Germany.

The Sudeten area was important to Czechoslovakia. It:

- contained important metals and mines
- bordered Germany and contained vital Czech defences, rendering the rest of Czechoslovakia defenceless without the Sudeten fortresses.

Czechoslovakia partially mobilized its military at the end of May 1938 when it appeared that Germany might attack. Germany did not attack, but it became aware that Czechoslovakia would fight.

■ International response

Unlike with Austria, the international community responded to the Sudeten Crisis because Czechoslovakia:

- had alliances
- possessed a modern, sizeable army
- contained important industries
- had only a minority German population, unlike Austria.

Adding the Sudeten region to Germany would expand its economy, allowing it to rearm at a quicker rate.

■ France

One of Czechoslovakia's alliances was a military alliance with France. However, France intended the alliance as a defence against German aggression. It had not intended to come to the aid of Czechoslovakia. In addition, France was not ready for confrontation with Germany and had no battle plans prepared to attack Germany in any event.

■ Soviet Union

In 1935, Czechoslovakia and the Soviet Union signed a mutual defence treaty. The Soviets expected the alliance to work in connection with the mutual assurance treaty they had with France. Therefore, the Soviet Union would assist Czechoslovakia only if France acted as well.

■ Britain

Leaders of Britain's government put pressure on the government of Czechoslovakia to agree to Henlein's demands because they:

- had some sympathy for the idea of Germans wanting to live in Germany
- were not willing to fight over Czechoslovakia.

■ A continuing crisis

By July, Hitler desired confrontation with Czechoslovakia:

- Germany sent a large military force to conduct military manoeuvres along the shared border with Czechoslovakia.
- Hitler ordered Henlein to prevent any internal, Czechoslovak agreement of the crisis.
- Henlein created a crisis.
- Hitler declared that Czechoslovakia planned to exterminate Germans living there.
- Hitler demanded the dismantling of Czechoslovakia.

On 13 September, British Prime Minister **Neville Chamberlain** met Hitler in Berlin. Afterwards, Chamberlain and French Prime Minister **Édouard Daladier** agreed that areas of Czechoslovakia containing a majority German population should be ceded to Germany. Initially, Czechoslovakia rejected the proposal, but then accepted it as the only way to prevent war.

Hitler immediately demanded that German troops occupy the Sudeten. Britain and France rejected these demands. War seemed imminent.

Although Hitler did not want war with Britain and France, he thought the two countries would not go to war for Czechoslovakia. He ordered the army to prepare an invasion for 1 October.

COMPARING AND CONTRASTING SOURCES

The following activity is designed to help you identify similarities and differences between sources.

● Similarities and differences should focus on significant knowledge, not basic statements, dates, and so on. Differences may identify significant knowledge in one source that is not found in the other source.

Read Source I and Source J below. Identify similarities and differences and record them in the table that follows the source material.

SOURCE I

Excerpt from a speech by Adolf Hitler given at the Sports Palace in Berlin, 26 September 1938, published in *The French Yellow Book* located at The Avalon Project: Documents in Law, History and Diplomacy, Lillian Goldman Law Library, Yale Law School, New Haven, Connecticut, USA, published online. http://avalon.law.yale.edu/wwii/ylbk011.asp

And now we are confronted with the last problem which must be solved and which shall be solved. It is the last territorial claim which I have to make in Europe, but it is a claim from which I will not swerve, and which I will satisfy, God willing … I have but few things to say. I am grateful to Mr. Chamberlain for all his efforts, and I assured him that the German people want nothing but peace; but I also told him that I cannot extend any further the limits of our patience. I assured him, moreover, and I repeat it here, that when this problem is solved, there will be no more territorial problems for Germany in Europe; and I further assured him that from the moment when Czechoslovakia solves its problems, that is to say, when the Czechs have come to an arrangement with their other minorities, peacefully, without oppression, I shall no longer be interested in the Czech State. And this I guarantee. We don't want any Czechs at all.

SOURCE J

Excerpt from *Nazi Conspiracy and Aggression*, Volume I, compiled by the Office of the United States Chief of Counsel for Prosecution of Axis Criminality, published by the United States Printing Office, Washington, DC, USA, 1946, pp. 516–17. The book is a collection of evidence and guiding material prepared by the British and American prosecuting staff at the International Military Tribunal held in Nuremberg, better known as the Nuremberg Trials, in the prosecution of accused Nazi war criminals.

On 21 April 1938, Hitler and Keitel discussed the pretexts which Germany might develop to serve as an excuse for a sudden and overwhelming attack [on Czechoslovakia]. They considered the provocation of a period of diplomatic squabbling which, growing more serious, would lead to the excuse for war. In the alternative, and this alternative they found to be preferable, they planned to unleash a lightning attack as the result of an 'incident' of their own creation. Consideration was given to the assassination of the German Ambassador at Prague to create the requisite incident … Problems of transport and tactics were discussed with a view to overcoming all Czechoslovak resistance within four days, thus presenting the world with a fait accompli and forestalling outside intervention. Thus in mid-April 1938 the designs of the Nazi conspirators to conquer Czechoslovakia had already reached the stage of practical planning.

This conspiracy must be viewed against a background of amicable German–Czech diplomatic relations. Although they had in the fall of 1937 determined to destroy the Czechoslovak State, the leaders of the German government were bound by a treaty of arbitration and by assurances freely given to observe the sovereignty of Czechoslovakia. By a formal treaty signed at Locarno on 16 October 1925, Germany and Czechoslovakia agreed, with certain exceptions, to refer to an arbitral tribunal or to the Permanent Court of International Justice … Formal and categoric assurances of their good will toward Czechoslovakia were forthcoming from the Nazi conspirators as late as March 1938. On 11 and 12 March 1938, at the time of the annexation of Austria, Germany had a considerable interest in inducing Czechoslovakia not to mobilize. At this time Goering assured M. Mastny, the Czechoslovak Minister in Berlin, on behalf of the German Government that German–Czech relations were not adversely affected by the developments in Austria and that Germany had no hostile intentions toward Czechoslovakia.

	Source C	Source B
Similarity 1		
Similarity 2		
Similarity 3		

	Source C	Source B
Difference 1		
Difference 2		
Difference 3		

WRITING A COMPARE AND CONTRAST RESPONSE

Take the information from the table from the activity above and write a response to the question below. Review the examples of effective sentence structures given below before writing your response. A focused response will consist of six statements, one per similarity or difference. It also will completely address one demand, compare for example, before addressing the other demand, contrast.

Sample sentence structures for comparing and contrasting sources

Comparing
- **Both Source C and Source D …**
- **Source C identifies … so does Source D with '…'**
- **Source D claims … similarly Source C states …**

Contrasting
- **Source C emphasizes … but Source D focuses on …**
- **While Source C asserts … . Source D claims …**
- **Source D examines … . On the other hand, Source C refers to …**

14 Compare and contrast what Source I and Source J inform us about the Sudeten Crisis.

■ Munich Agreement, 30 September 1938

The threat of war worried Mussolini because Italy was not militarily prepared. He called for a meeting with Hitler, Chamberlain and Daladier. Leaders of Czechoslovakia and the Soviet Union were not invited. The four leaders met in Munich and reached an agreement on 30 September. Terms of the Munich Agreement included:

- The Sudeten would become part of Germany.
- German troops would occupy the Sudeten in stages.
- A plebiscite would determine which country residents preferred.
- Germans would be released from Czechoslovakian military service.

Czechoslovakia had little choice but to accept these terms. Britain and France stated that they would not fight Germany if Czechoslovakia did not abide by the agreement.

■ Results of the Sudeten Crisis

Also on 30 September, Germany and Britain announced the Anglo-German Declaration. The two countries pledged to consult one another over potential conflicts and vowed not to go to war.

■ France

The Munich Agreement was popular in France. However, it left France less secure:

- The power of Czechoslovakia, a major ally, was diminished.
- France's abandonment of the mutual assistance guarantee damaged relations with the Soviet Union.
- Britain continued to refuse military alliance with France.

In November 1938, France increased military spending by 300%. A Franco-German Declaration pledge to respect borders and pursue peace was signed in December 1938.

■ Britain

The Munich Agreement also was popular in Britain. Chamberlain had brought peace to Europe. However, there were concerns:

- A weakened France might seek an agreement to avoid conflict with Germany.
- Britain had no reliable ally.
- Germany had come close to going to war, indicating that Germany saw war as a way to address its grievances or resolve its demands.

Britain increased the speed of its rearmament.

■ Soviet Union

The Soviet Union could not trust Britain and France to join them in case of a German attack. Because the two countries seemed to favour fascist states like Germany and Italy, the Soviets believed the two countries might join Germany in a war against the Soviet Union. The Soviet Union was isolated.

■ Germany

Hitler had been willing to go to war with Czechoslovakia, but not Britain and France. After the annexation of the Sudeten, the German military realized the strength of Czechoslovakia's defences. Victory would not have been easy. A plot developed among military leaders to assassinate Hitler and end Nazi rule.

However, the Munich Agreement made Hitler immensely popular in Germany. Concerned about the public's reaction to an assassination, the military ended the plot.

Between 2 October and 20 November, Czechoslovakia was dismantled by Slovaks, Hungary, Poland and Germany. Only a rump state remained.

On 14 March 1939, Hitler threatened Czechoslovakian President Emil Hácha. Hitler gave Hácha two options:

- agree to make Czechoslovakia part of Germany, or
- Germany would invade.

A large part of Czechoslovakia became part of Germany. Slovakia was separated from the rest of the former state and became an independent country, as well as a German ally.

The hopes for peace from the Munich Agreement were gone in only six months.

SUMMARIZING A SOURCE

- Question 12 of Paper 1 requires students to integrate knowledge from four sources and their own understanding in response to a question about a topic from one of the case studies in The move to global war.
- A successful response requires students to integrate summaries of sources.
- A good summary is based on the main ideas of a source. The main idea of a source can be identified using relevant content or identifying how relevant content is connected by a bigger idea or concept.
- The question is worth 9 marks. It is the most valuable question and you should devote the most time to answering it.
- You should spend 30–35 minutes answering the question. It is recommended that the first five to eight minutes be used to outline your response. You should spend the last 25 minutes writing the essay.

With reference to Source K, complete the table below. After completing the table, write a one- to two-sentence summary of Source K.

SOURCE K

Excerpt from *Hitler's Generals*, edited by Correlli Barnett, published by Grove Press, New York, USA, 1989, p. 6. Barnett is a military and economic historian and former professor at Cambridge University, UK.

By means of his 'shop-window' rearmament and his well-tuned rantings about the terrors that would ensue if Germany were not accorded her just deserts, Hitler achieved his greatest diplomatic triumph at Munich in 1938, when Chamberlain persuaded France to abandon her ally Czechoslovakia, and the two democracies handed him the Sudetenland, which happened to contain the powerful Czech frontier defences. The Munich Agreement radically altered the strategic balance of Europe in Hitler's favour, opening the way to his final occupation of Czechoslovakia in March 1939, which in turn uncovered the southern flank of his next victim, Poland. But Munich marked not only Hitler's triumph over Chamberlain and Daladier, but also over the leadership of the German Army.

Importance of the Munich Agreement	
Relevant content	One idea connecting relevant content
Hitler handed the Sudetenland	
Strategic balance altered	
Occupation of Czechoslovakia	
Poland becomes vulnerable	
Hitler triumphs over leadership of German Army	

SUMMARIZING A SOURCE

SOURCE L

Excerpt from the Franco-German Declaration of 6 December 1938, located at the Avalon Project: Documents in Law, History and Diplomacy, which is sponsored by Yale Law School, New Haven, Connecticut, USA.

Acting in the name and by order of their respective Governments, [ministers] agreed on the following points at their meeting in Paris on December 6, 1938:

1. The French Government and the German Government fully share the conviction that pacific and neighbourly relations between France and Germany constitute one of the essential elements of the consolidation of the situation in Europe and of the preservation of peace. Consequently both Governments will endeavour [work] with all their might to assure the development of the relations between their countries in this direction.

2. Both Governments agree that no question of a territorial nature remains in suspense [unresolved] between their countries and solemnly recognize as permanent the frontier between their countries as it is actually drawn.

3. Both Governments are resolved, without prejudice to their special relations with Third Powers, to remain in contact on all questions of importance to both their countries and to have recourse to mutual consultation in case any complications arising out of these questions should threaten to lead to international difficulties.

15 With reference to Source L above, highlight the sentence or part of a sentence, in the paragraphs numbered 1–3, that best summarizes the main point of each paragraph. After completing the highlighting, write a one- to two-sentence summary of Source J.

The final crisis and outbreak of war 1939

After successfully annexing Austria and Czechoslovakia, Germany turned its attention to Poland. At the Paris Peace Conference, Poland was created partially using German land. The desire to regain the Free City of Danzig and the Polish Corridor, which separated Germany from the German territory of East Prussia, influenced German actions.

■ Polish Crisis 1938–9

After the occupation of the Sudeten, Germany entered talks with Poland to:

- build transportation links with East Prussia
- enter a 25-year non-aggression pact with Poland
- help Poland gain territory elsewhere.

In October 1938, Hitler demanded the return of Danzig:

- Danzig had been part of Germany until the end of the First World War.
- The locally elected government of Danzig was dominated by the Nazi Party.

German demands for Danzig created popular outrage in Britain and France. It was thought Germany's territorial demands had ended with the Munich Agreement. The British and French governments were pressured not to give in to German demands. Britain also worried that France might negotiate a security agreement with Germany. In February 1939, Britain announced military support for France.

■ Guarantee of Poland's borders, March 1939

Poland declared no interest in negotiating. Poland informed the League of Nations that it would go to war if Germany tried to annex Danzig. On 31 March 1939, Britain and France guaranteed Poland's borders. The guarantee strengthened Poland's resolve not to negotiate.

The combined military production of Britain and France would be greater than Germany's by autumn 1939.

Britain began creating an anti-fascist network of alliances. It signed mutual assistance agreements with Greece, Romania, Albania and Turkey.

Despite their guarantees, Britain and France refused to give Poland military and financial assistance.

■ Britain and France negotiate with the Soviet Union

Britain and France proposed that the Soviet Union join their anti-fascist coalition. They argued that Soviet support of Poland would prevent a German attack.

- Britain and France pledged to maintain the current borders of eastern Europe.
- The Soviet Union had lost territory in eastern Europe after the First World War, including the Baltic states, Finland, Poland and part of Romania.
- The Soviet Union wanted these territories restored to them.

Poland absolutely refused permission for Soviet forces to enter its territory.

The Soviet Union was not impressed. Without permission to enter Poland, the German army would be on the Soviet border before they could be fought. In addition, Britain and France sent low-level diplomats to negotiate with the Soviet Union. The Soviets came to understand that they were not legitimate allies for Britain and France, only a tool to be used.

■ Germany's response

Britain and France had not shown resolve during the Sudeten Crisis. Hitler believed they would not go to war for Poland. Shortly after Poland's borders were guaranteed, Hitler ordered the army to develop an invasion plan for Poland, called Case White. On 28 April, Germany withdrew from the Polish–German Non-Aggression Pact.

SUMMARIZING A SOURCE

- Question 12 of Paper 1 requires students to integrate knowledge from four sources and their own understanding in response to a question about a topic from one of the case studies in The move to global war.
- A successful response requires students to integrate summaries of sources.
- A good summary is based upon the main ideas of a source. The main idea of a source can be identified using relevant content or identifying how relevant content is connected by a bigger idea or concept.
- The question is worth 9 marks. It is the most valuable question and you should devote the most time to answering it.
- You should spend 30–35 minutes answering the question. It is recommended that the first five to eight minutes be used to outline your response. You should spend the last 25 minutes writing the essay.

With reference to Source M, complete the table below. After completing the table, write a one- to two-sentence summary of Source M.

SOURCE M

Excerpt from *The Road to War* by Richard Overy and Andrew Wheatcroft, published by Penguin Books, London, UK, 1999, pp. 64–5. Overy is a prominent modern historian and professor at Exeter University, UK. Wheatcroft is a professor at City University London, UK.

On 3 April Hitler definitely resolved to attack Poland and bring the disputed territories, rich in coal and agricultural resources into the Greater Reich [German Empire] by force. On 23 May he called the military together again to his study in the Chancellery [office]. 'The Pole is not a fresh enemy,' he told them, 'Poland will always be on the side of our adversaries … It is not Danzig that is at stake. For us it is a matter of expanding our living-space in the east and making food supplies secure' …

… The war could be isolated only, Hitler continued, as 'a matter of skilful politic'. His experience of Western appeasement in 1938 convinced him that neither Britain nor France would seriously fight for Poland. This conviction dominated Hitler's thinking throughout the crisis which led to war. The decision to attack Poland can only be understood in the light of this conviction. The war with the West, if it came, would come not in 1939, but in three or four years as planned, 'when the armaments programme will be completed' …

… Hitler saw the contest with the West as a contest of wills: 'Our enemies have men who are below average. No personalities. No masters, men of action … Our enemies are little worms. I saw them in Munich.' Democracy had made the west soft.

Basis of Hitler's resolve to attack Poland	
Relevant content	One idea connecting relevant content
Expanding living space and securing food supply	
Western appeasement	
Contest of wills	
Democracy made the west soft	

SUMMARIZING A SOURCE

With reference to Source N, answer the questions below. After answering the questions, write a one- to two-sentence summary of Source N.

SOURCE N

Excerpt from *The History of Poland* by M.B. Biskupski, published by Greenwood Press, Connecticut, USA, 2000, p. 93. Biskupski is a prominent historian on central European affairs at Central Connecticut State University, USA.

In the last months of peace, the Germans and the Western powers pursued some understanding with the Soviets in anticipation of imminent hostilities: the Germans to avoid a major conflict in the east and to isolate Poland, assuming Western inactions; the allies to pressure Hitler with so daunting a prospect of a two-front war he would quail, or, if the worst came, have a major eastern foe in the form of the Soviet Union. For their part, the Soviets hoped for mutually destructive struggle among capitalist states and had little interest in rescuing despised Poland. Soviet negotiations with the West were pointless from the start and were conducted in bad faith. The Soviet insistence that their troops be allowed complete discretion to enter Polish territory should they join against the Germans, which the Poles rejected as compromising their sovereignty, was never a serious issue despite the attention later given to it by many historians. The Soviets raised the issue merely to draw the Western powers, isolate Poland, and up the ante in their simultaneous negotiations with Germany.

16 What was the ultimate goal of Soviet actions during the crisis in Poland in 1939?

17 What was the goal of the Soviet Union's negotiations with the Nazis and the west?

18 How did the Germans and the west assist the Soviets in achieving better terms in negotiating with the Nazis?

■ Pact of Steel, May 1939

Pressure from Britain and France led Germany to create a formal alliance with Italy, known as the Pact of Steel. The terms of the agreement included:

● closer co-ordination of foreign policies, the press and propaganda
● supporting each other in war
● developing war plans together.

The historian A.J.P. Taylor argued that Germany never intended to carry out these terms and used the Pact of Steel to increase pressure on Britain and France. Germany hoped to instil fear of a larger war.

■ Nazi–Soviet Pact, 23 August 1939

On 23 August 1939, after secret negotiations, Germany and the Soviet Union signed the Treaty of Non-Aggression between Germany and the Soviet Union, better known as the Nazi–Soviet Pact. The two countries agreed:

● not to fight one another
● to give Germany freedom in diplomacy
● that areas in Poland that once belonged to Russia would be reabsorbed into the Soviet Union.

Germany no longer had to fear Soviet intervention in Poland.

■ Invasion of Poland, 1 September 1939

During the crisis, Britain and France hoped Poland would grant Germany's demands. Poland continued to refuse to negotiate. Britain and France maintained their support of Poland.

■ Mobilization, 21 August 1939

On 21 August, Hitler ordered the military to mobilize for the invasion of Poland. The invasion, Case White, was scheduled for 26 August.

■ Invasion delayed, 25 August 1939

On 25 August, Hitler delayed the invasion because of two developments:

● Britain and Poland announced a military alliance.
● Mussolini stated that Italy was not prepared for war and could not abide by the Pact of Steel.

The Pact of Steel was modified to allow Italy to support Germany in other than military ways.

On 25 and 26 August, talks between Germany, Britain and France failed to reach an agreement.

On 28 August, Britain issued a formal warning to Germany not to violate Poland's borders. Britain also ordered:

● British ships in the Baltic and Mediterranean Seas to leave their bases in case of surprise attack.
● Implementation of emergency rationing of food and essential supplies in Britain.

These moves did not convince Hitler that Britain would go to war.

On 31 August, Hitler met the Polish ambassador in Berlin. Hitler demanded the return of Danzig and added a new demand: the return of the Polish Corridor. The Polish ambassador did not have the authority to sign a treaty. Germany announced that Poland had rejected negotiations.

■ Poland invaded, 1 September

On 1 September, a massive force of more than 1.5 million German troops invaded Poland.

■ International response to the invasion of Poland

Britain and France called for an end to hostilities. An Italian call for a conference of world powers to resolve the crisis was ignored.

Britain and France declared war on Germany on 3 September 1939. Accounts indicate that Hitler was shocked by the declaration of war. A localized war between Germany and Poland turned into a European war. The war that would become the Second World War in Europe and north Africa had started.

MIND MAP

Use the information from the opposite page to add details to the mind map below.

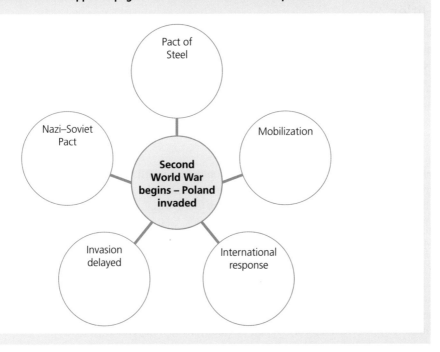

PERSPECTIVE

- Perspective is a particular way of regarding or understanding historical understanding.
- It is most commonly understood as an interpretation of historical events or understanding.
- All historical topics can be seen from multiple perspectives or interpretations.
- Only through examining multiple perspectives can a historian develop deeper understanding of the past.
- Understanding perspective for Paper 1 can be used in responding to all four questions found on Paper 1.

Use the details from your mind map above to develop your perspective on the short-term causes of the Second World War. Then read Source O below and identify the perspective on the short-term causes of the Second World War. Complete the table that follows the source with evidence that supports the perspective from each source.

SOURCE O

Excerpt from 'Poland Caused WW II: Russian Report' by Mike Eckel, published in *The World Post*, July 2009. *The World Post* is an online news source and is associated with the Berggruen Institute of Governance. In this article, US-based reporter Eckel quotes Colonel Sergei Kovalyov, a member of the Institute of Military History of Russia, a section of the Russian Ministry of Defence.

'Everyone who has studied the history of World War II without bias knows that the war began because of Poland's refusal to satisfy Germany's claims,' he writes.

Kovalyov called the demands 'quite reasonable.' He observed: 'The overwhelming majority of residents of Danzig, cut off from Germany by the Treaty of Versailles, were Germans who sincerely wished for the reunification with their historical homeland.'

	Perspective on short-term causes of war	Evidence supporting the perspective
Your perspective from the mind map above		
Perspective of Source O		

Key debate

■ Germany and Hitler

A.J.P. Taylor argued that blaming Hitler was too simplistic. He viewed Hitler's foreign policy as an expansion of earlier German foreign policies and other states throughout history. Taylor claimed that Hitler was blamed because he was German and dead.

Many historians, however, blamed Hitler for causing the Second World War. These historians see Hitler as playing a personal role in shaping the *Anschluss*, Sudeten Crisis, Munich Agreement, mobilization of German forces and the decision to invade Poland.

■ Poland

Some historians place blame on Poland's refusal to negotiation or compromise with Germany's demands. The Polish Corridor and Danzig contained many German residents, who experienced discrimination. Many of these residents probably wanted to be part of Germany.

A.J.P. Taylor and historian Richard Overy contend that many Germans desired the return of Danzig and the Polish Corridor. Hitler was under great political pressure to regain these territories.

■ Britain

Richard Overy places blame on Britain and France. He believes they used appeasement to preserve their status as world powers. Britain and France viewed their acceptance of Germany's reasonable demands as a form of permission by the Great Powers. When Germany acted independently, Britain and France reacted because it was a challenge to their authority.

P.M.H. Bell places some responsibility on Britain for guaranteeing Poland's border as a cause of the Second World War. The guarantee was a challenge to Germany, making war more likely.

A.J.P. Taylor blames Britain and France for transforming a local war between Germany and Poland into a wider war when they declared war on Germany two days after Germany's invasion of Poland.

■ A note on the work of historians

The complexities of history like those causing the Second World War lead to multiple interpretations. The historians mentioned above agree any many aspects of causation of the Second World War. However, the significance they place on particular pieces of evidence develops different interpretations. Such debates and disagreements on the causes of the Second World War will continue into the future.

PERSPECTIVE

- Perspective is a particular way of regarding or understanding historical understanding.
- It is most commonly understood as an interpretation of historical events or understanding.
- All historical topics can be seen from multiple perspectives or interpretations.
- Only through examining multiple perspectives can a historian develop deeper understanding of the past.
- Understanding perspective for Paper 1 can be used in responding to all four questions found on Paper 1.

Read Source P and Source Q below and identify the perspective found in each source. Complete the table that follows the source with evidence that supports the perspective from each source.

SOURCE P

Excerpt from *The Origin of the Second World War* by A.J.P. Taylor, published by Penguin Books, London, UK, 1991, pp. 26–7. Taylor was a British historian who wrote many books on European history and was a lecturer at many British universities.

Little can be discovered so long as we go on attributing everything that happened to Hitler … He would have counted for nothing without the support and cooperation of the German people. It seems to be believed nowadays that Hitler did everything himself, even driving the trains and filling the gas chambers unaided. That was not so. Hitler was a sounding-board for the German nation. Thousands, many hundred thousands, of Germans carried out his evil orders without qualm or question. As supreme ruler of Germany, Hitler bears the greatest responsibility for acts in immeasurable evil: for the destruction of German democracy, for the concentration camps; and worst of all, for the extermination of peoples during the Second World War … His foreign policy was a different matter. He aimed to make Germany the dominant Power in Europe and maybe, more remotely, in the world. Other Powers have pursued similar aims, and still do. Other Powers treat smaller countries as their satellites. Other Powers seek to defend their vital interests by force of arms. In international affairs there was nothing wrong with Hitler except that he was German.

SOURCE Q

Excerpt from *1939: Countdown to War* by Richard Overy, published by Allen Lane, London, UK, 2009, p. 117. Overy is a prominent twentieth-century historian who is a professor of history at Exeter University, UK.

The British and French decision for war has also to be seen against the background of growing fears in both populations that Germany in particular represented a profound threat to their existing way of life and the values that they wished to see observed in the conduct of international affairs. Although it is often argued, and with justice, that neither state cared very much to observe these values in the treatment of their empires, the two powers saw themselves as self-appointed guardians of a Western world assailed by internal anxiety and external threat. In Britain in particular there existed a strong sense of responsibility for keeping the wider world in order. 'Great Britain', wrote the politician Oliver Harvey in April 1939, in a wide ranging survey of the international order, 'is the greatest, richest and potentially strongest Power' and should use that power to restore sanity to the world.

	Perspective on causes of war	Evidence supporting the perspective
Perspective of Source P		
Perspective of Source Q		

INTEGRATING KNOWLEDGE AND SOURCES

- Question 12 of Paper 1 requires students to integrate knowledge from four sources and their own understanding in response to a question about a topic from one of the case studies in The move to global war.
- The question is worth 9 marks. It is the most valuable question and you should devote the most time to answering it.
- You should spend 30–35 minutes answering the question. It is recommended that the first five to eight minutes be used to outline your response. You should spend the last 25 minutes writing the essay.

Using Sources A–Q found in Chapter 4, identify relevant content to help answer the following question:

Examine German foreign policy 1933–40 on the road to war.

Record a brief summary of the relevant content from each source in a table.

Source booklet

Read Sources A–D below and answer questions 9–12 in the accompanying question paper.

SOURCE A

Excerpt from *Hitler's Generals*, edited by Correlli Barnett, published by Grove Press, New York, USA, 1989, p. 6. Barnett is a military and economic historian and former professor at Cambridge University, UK.

By means of his 'shop-window' rearmament and his well-tuned rantings about the terrors that would ensue if Germany were not accorded her just deserts, Hitler achieved his greatest diplomatic triumph at Munich in 1938, when Chamberlain persuaded France to abandon her ally Czechoslovakia, and the two democracies handed him the Sudetenland, which happened to contain the powerful Czech frontier defences. The Munich Agreement radically altered the strategic balance of Europe in Hitler's favour, opening the way to his final occupation of Czechoslovakia in March 1939, which in turn uncovered the southern flank of his next victim, Poland. But Munich marked not only Hitler's triumph over Chamberlain and Daladier, but also over the leadership of the German Army.

SOURCE B

A political cartoon by the political cartoonist David Low titled 'Someone is taking someone for a walk', published 21 October 1939 in the *Evening Standard* newspaper.

SOMEONE IS TAKING SOMEONE FOR A WALK

SOURCE C

Excerpt from *The Origin of the Second World War* by A.J.P. Taylor, published by Penguin Books, UK, 1991, pp. 26–7. Taylor was a British historian who wrote many books on European history and was a lecturer at many British universities.

Little can be discovered so long as we go on attributing everything that happened to Hitler … He would have counted for nothing without the support and cooperation of the German people. It seems to be believed nowadays that Hitler did everything himself, even driving the trains and filling the gas chambers unaided. That was not so. Hitler was a sounding-board for the German nation. Thousands, many hundred thousands, of Germans carried out his evil orders without qualm or question. As supreme ruler of Germany, Hitler bears the greatest responsibility for acts in immeasurable evil: for the destruction of German democracy, for the concentration camps; and worst of all, for the extermination of peoples during the Second World War … His foreign policy was a different matter. He aimed to make Germany the dominant Power in Europe and maybe, more remotely, in the world. Other Powers have pursued similar aims, and still do. Other Powers treat smaller countries as their satellites. Other Powers seek to defend their vital interests by force of arms. In international affairs there was nothing wrong with Hitler except that he was German.

SOURCE D

Excerpt from *The Road to War* by Richard Overy and Andrew Wheatcroft, published by Penguin Books, London, UK, 1999, pp. 64–5. Overy is a prominent modern historian and professor at Exeter University, UK. Wheatcroft is a professor at City University, London, UK.

On 3 April Hitler definitely resolved to attack Poland and bring the disputed territories, rich in coal and agricultural resources into the Greater Reich [German Empire] by force. On 23 May he called the military together again to his study in the Chancellery [office]. 'The Pole is not a fresh enemy,' he told them, 'Poland will always be on the side of our adversaries … It is not Danzig that is at stake. For us it is a matter of expanding our living-space in the east and making food supplies secure' …

… The war could be isolated only, Hitler continued, as 'a matter of skilful politic.' His experience of Western appeasement in 1938 convinced him that neither Britain nor France would seriously fight for Poland. This conviction dominated Hitler's thinking throughout the crisis which led to war. The decision to attack Poland can only be understood in the light of this conviction. The war with the West, if it came, would come not in 1939, but in three or four years as planned, 'when the armaments programme will be completed' …

… Hitler saw the contest with the West as a contest of wills: 'Our enemies have men who are below average. No personalities. No masters, men of action … Our enemies are little worms. I saw them in Munich.' Democracy had made the west soft.

Sample questions and answers

Below are sample answers. Read them and the comments around them.

9a According to Source A, what were the effects of the Munich Agreement?

> Hitler's 'shop window' armament and his terrorizing rants effected the outcome of the Munich Agreement.
>
> The Munich Agreement changed the strategic balance by making Germany stronger. •——— Good example of paraphrasing.
>
> Hitler gained power over the leaders of his army.

2/3. The second and third responses are good summaries of the main points from the excerpt. They result in the award of 2 marks. The first response, however, seems to suffer from a misunderstanding of the words 'effect' and 'affect'. 'Effect' refers to the result of some action or change. The question uses this definition, meaning that responses should focus on developments that occurred because or as a result of the Munich Agreement. The first response refers to developments prior to the Munich Agreement and identifies some causes of Hitler's success in Munich. The response uses the word 'effect' instead of the word 'affect'. 'Affect' refers to factors that influence or cause a change, which can be called an effect. The meanings of these two words are often confused by students. The best way to remember which meaning goes with which word is to remember the sequence of events is the same as the sequence of the beginning letters of each word in the alphabet. 'A' comes first, similar to an affect which is a cause of an event that resulted in change. 'E' comes after 'a' in the alphabet, just like an effect is the result of change that happened after an event.

9b What message is conveyed in Source B?

> Hitler and Stalin are taking a friendly walk on the Eastern Frontier.
>
> Both men are carrying guns, signifying that they do not trust each other.

1/2. The first response is descriptive. It does not state a message. The second response, however, identifies one of the key messages. Stalin and Hitler are walking on the 'eastern frontier', which means this is after Poland had been occupied by both the Soviet Union and Germany. The agreement they made helped both of them in the short term, but now each was tied to an enemy they could not trust.

10 With reference to its origin, purpose and content, evaluate the value and limitations of Source C for a historian studying German foreign policy 1933–40.

> The source is a book written by A.J.P. Taylor. Because it is a secondary source, it used a wider range of research material than a primary source. This made it possible for a deeper analysis. However, it may not have the same depth of knowledge that a primary source has, such as if it were a speech by Hitler. The excerpt criticizes putting full blame for everything in Nazi Germany on Hitler, especially foreign policy. It also is good because Taylor was an expert historian. It also could have been better if it had more specific examples of German foreign policy.

This is a description with implied evaluation. Using one of the OPCVL terms in the sentence would have made it an explicit evaluation and more likely to connect the description to a deeper evaluation.

This an example of describing content without connecting it to either value or limitation.

2/4. The response is inconsistent in its development of its evaluation of origin, purpose, content, value and limitations. A brief reference to origin is made with the first sentence, but it is limited in its development of origin. There is one clear reference to content regarding blame, but this content is not connected to an evaluation of value or limitation. It describes content, but does not evaluate it. The last sentence may be an attempt to evaluate the limitations of content, but it is not clear given the use of the phrase 'could have been better'. Why was it not as good as possible? What would have made it better? Similarly, the evaluation of value is limited. Stating that secondary sources use a wider range of evidence providing deeper analysis is one reason such sources have value. However, it is a generic statement that could be applied to any secondary source and does not fully evaluate Source C in the context of question 10. The statement that Taylor was an expert historian is a reference to value, but it is not made explicit. There is no reference to purpose in the response. This is an example of what can happen when the specific terms origin, purpose, content, value and limitation are not used and underlined in the response. Had this technique been used, a quick review of the response would have identified the omission. Finally, using the terms in the response helps with organization and clarity, as well as including an evaluation instead of a description of value and limitation.

11 Compare and contrast what Source A and Source D reveal about German foreign policy, 1933–40.

Both Source A and Source D make reference to Hitler's political domination of the western leaders, with Source A specifically naming Chamberlain and Daladier. Where Source A identifies the reasons for Hitler's diplomatic successes in its first sentence, Source D focuses mostly on how these diplomatic successes affected Hitler's thinking and their impact on his strategy. An example of this is Hitler's belief that Britain and France would not go to war over Poland, which is similar to the events of the Munich Agreement from Source A where Britain and France did not risk fighting for Czechoslovakia, causing a radical change in the strategic balance in Europe. Both sources also indicate Hitler's desire to expand his power into Poland. Source D focuses on Hitler's intentions to go to war, whereas Source A concentrates on international relations and diplomacy.

Effective summary of political domination found in both sources.

The transition here '[a]n example of this ... ' makes it difficult to quickly identify whether the sentence is a similarity or a difference. Use two separate paragraphs, one for similarities and one for differences.

Uses conjunctions that show difference such as 'whereas'.

4/6. The response identifies several similarities and differences. However, it does not identify six of them. There are three similarities stated, but only two differences. One reason for this oversight is the response's organization. Instead of using one paragraph each for similarities and differences, these statements are intermixed into one paragraph. There seems to be an attempt to create one cohesive paragraph where sentences use transitions based on topics. This may be the reason for the claim that Hitler did not think Britain and France would go to war over Czechoslovakia. It is a logical inference, but does not seem to be the context used in Source A by Barnett. However, the last statement is a good example of using perspective in a compare and contrast question. The response also makes it easy to identify usage of sources.

12 Using these sources and your own knowledge, to what extent did German foreign policy cause the tensions leading to the Second World War?

The command term 'to what extent' means to '[c]onsider the merits or otherwise of an argument or concept. Opinions and conclusions should be presented clearly and supported with appropriate evidence and sound argument' (History Guide, first examinations 2017, p. 97).

German foreign policy was a significant factor in creating the tensions that led to the Second World War. However, the foreign policy of countries like Britain, France and the Soviet Union played some role as well.

A.J.P. Taylor claimed Hitler 'aimed to make Germany the dominant Power in Europe and maybe, more remotely, in the world' (Source C). For a country to move from a position of limited power, like Germany was after the First World War, to try to dominate other countries can only result in increased tensions. Even though Britain and France tried to negotiate with Hitler in Munich, it only resulted in changing 'the strategic balance of Europe' (Source A). The change refers to Germany's increased influence and power over Britain and France. Both these countries saw too late that Hitler would not stop with the Munich Agreement. They agreed to support Poland against Germany. As Source D shows, Poland was Hitler's next target and he intended to invade Poland. After Germany successfully invaded Poland, that created tensions between Germany and the Soviet Union as shown in Source B, where Hitler and Stalin are walking together but both of them hold guns because they do not trust each other. Every source from the exam booklet has an example of how German foreign policy helped increase international tensions leading up to the Second World War.

Hitler's foreign policy goals can be summed up into three specific aims: revise the Treaty of Versailles (ToV), make Germany the dominant power as Taylor claimed, and *lebensraum* or territorial expansion to the east. Revising the terms of the ToV was not a new German foreign policy goal. It had been one ever since the treaty had been signed. But, Hitler was the first to take significant actions that defied the treaty. He began German rearmament and conscription that would increase the size of the German army. He also remilitarized the Rhineland. No country did much in response, partially because they were dealing with the problems of the Great Depression. Similarly, the *Anschluss* with Austria violated the ToV, but there were no strong reactions from any major power. When he sought to bring the Sudetenland into Germany and threatened war with Czechoslovakia, Britain and France signed the Munich Agreement, giving Germany the Sudetenland. As both Sources A and D suggest, this was a major turning point in the balance of power. Hitler became certain that he would not be opposed as he prepared to occupy the rest of Czechoslovakia and then invade Poland. It was not until his actions in Czechoslovakia and with Poland that Britain and France began to seriously oppose Germany, increasing tensions that led to war.

As can be seen from the sources and outside knowledge, German foreign policy under Hitler became aggressive and changed international relations in Europe. However, serious tensions did not develop until the late 1930s. The Great Depression caused many problems for most countries that led them to focus more on domestic problems instead of foreign policy. As long as Hitler focused on returning Germans to Germany and revising the harsher terms of the ToV, no serious tensions threatened war. However, German foreign policy helped Germany become the largest military power in Europe and encouraged the pursuit of *lebensraum* or German expansion to the east. It was Hitler's actions to achieve *lebensraum* that caused the Second World War.

The response immediately answers the demands of the question.

Use of source labels helps assure that all sources have been used for both the writer and the examiner.

Own knowledge and source material are integrated.

Final paragraph summarizes the argument developed in previous paragraphs. However, it fails to address the claims from the introduction.

6/9. The response makes a good argument that addresses the demands of the question, but does not completely address the 'to what extent' demand. The introduction is strong and shows understanding of the demands of the question. It makes a definitive claim regarding 'to what extent' by declaring 'German foreign policy was a significant factor' and then claiming other powers played some roles as well. The first body paragraph is an excellent example of using all sources while also integrating own knowledge. It also demonstrates several effective methods to identify the use of source material. The response then goes on to effectively develop and support with relevant source knowledge and own knowledge the significant role of German foreign policy in creating tensions that led to the Second World War. However, as a 'to what extent' question, it is necessary to examine in some detail other factors in addressing the question. While the introduction asserts that the response will do so, there is no development of the role of Britain, France or the Soviet Union in creating tensions that led to war. While each of these three countries is identified in the response, it is always in the context of developing German foreign policy. There is no explicit development of the foreign policies or roles of Britain, France or the Soviet Union in causing the Second World War. Therefore, the demands of the question are only partially addressed. The response could have more effectively integrated source knowledge and own knowledge consistently throughout the whole response. The first body paragraph mostly focuses on source material and the second body paragraph mostly focuses on own knowledge.

Exam practice

Now it's your turn to take a mock exam.

Read Sources I–L below and answer questions 9–12 in the accompanying question paper. The sources and questions relate to Case study 2: Italian and German expansion 1933–40.

SOURCE I

Excerpt from *The Origin of the Second World War in Europe*, second edition by P.M.H. Bell, published by Pearson Education, London, UK, 1998, p. 158. Bell is an honorary senior fellow at the Department of History at the University of Liverpool, UK, and has published several books.

… he [Schacht] introduced his 'New Plan' for German foreign trade, based on the principles of buying nothing that could not be paid for by foreign exchange earned by German exports, and of making imports conform to national needs as decided by the government. All imports were subject to licences, which were used to differentiate between essential and non-essential items, with raw materials and food classified as essential. Whenever possible, imports were to be bought only from the countries which were willing to accept German goods in return; and any foreign exchange involved was to be paid into a clearing account, and not used freely by the exporting country.

SOURCE J

From an election campaign flyer 'This Has Been Achieved,' for the Reichstag elections of 29 March 1936, a referendum to approve of the reoccupation of the Rhineland. The chart shows the increase in industrial production in terms of billions of marks. The caption reads: 'There are no idle machines any longer in factories and plants! National Socialism does not give up, it attacks. The value of industrial production grew by 23½ billion marks, which is 67%.'

SOURCE K

Excerpt from 'The Nazi Economy – Was It Geared to War?' by Richard Overy, published in *History Review*, No. 31, September 1998. *History Review* was a major journal devoted to publishing authoritative articles by modern historians; it ended in 2012. Overy is a prominent historian and a history professor at Exeter University, UK.

… The armed forces themselves were anxious to rebuild German military power cautiously, step-by-step, so that they could control its pace and character themselves. The first priority here was to build the infrastructure of military life – barracks, airfields, training schools – that had been shut down or destroyed during the period of enforced disarmament. The first air force production programmes were largely devoted to building trainer aircraft. Between 1934 and 1938 some 58 per cent of aircraft production was made up of trainer aircraft and only 18 per cent of combat planes. Tank production was slow to get going and the programme for naval shipbuilding laid down in March 1934 had achieved little before the late 1930s. Remilitarization on any scale took time to achieve because Germany began in 1933 from a very low base.

SOURCE L

Excerpt from *Nazi Conspiracy and Aggression*, Volume 1, published by Office of the United States Chief of Counsel for Prosecution of Axis Criminality, 1946. This is one book of a 12-volume series more commonly known as the 'Red Series' and consists of documentary evidence used by the US and British prosecution staffs at the International Military Tribunal in Nuremberg, Germany, located online at the Avalon Project: Documents in Law, History and Diplomacy, which is sponsored by Yale Law School, New Haven, Connecticut, USA. http://avalon.law.yale.edu/imt/chap_08.asp

It must be emphasized that the secret rearmament program was launched immediately upon the seizure of power by the Nazi conspirators. On 4 April 1933 the Reich Cabinet passed a resolution establishing a Reich Defense Council. The function of this council was secretly to mobilize for war. At the second meeting of the working committee of the Councillors for Reich Defense, the predecessor of the Reich Defense Council, which was held on 22 May 1933, the chairman was [future Field Marshal Wilhelm] Keitel. Keitel stated that the Reich Defense Council would immediately undertake to prepare for war emergency. He stressed the urgency of the task of organizing a war economy, and announced that the council stood ready to brush aside all obstacles. Fully aware of the fact that their action was in flagrant violation of the Treaty of Versailles, Keitel emphasized the extreme importance of absolute secrecy … Detailed measures of financing a future war were discussed and it was pointed out that the financial aspects of the war economy would be regulated by the Reich Finance Ministry and the Reichsbank, which was headed by [Minister of Economics Hjalmar] Schacht.

Under his secret appointment as plenipotentiary-General of the War Economy, Schacht had the express function of placing all economic forces of the nation in the services of the Nazi war machine. The secret defense law of 21 May 1935 in effect gave Schacht charge of the entire war economy. In case of war he was to be virtual economic dictator of Germany. His task was to place all economic forces into service for the conduct of war and to secure economically the life of the German people …. He was to be responsible for the financing as well as for the conduct of the war; and he was further authorized to issue ordinances within his sphere of responsibility, even if these deviated from existing laws.

9 a What, according to Source I, were the directives of the 'New Plan'?   [3]

   b What is the message conveyed in Source J?   [2]

10 With reference to its origin, purpose and content, analyse the value and limitations of Source L for a historian studying economics and German foreign policy, 1933–40.   [4]

11 Compare and contrast how Source K and Source L describe economic policies and remilitarization in Nazi Germany.   [6]

12 Using the sources and your own knowledge, to what extent did Germany's foreign policy goals affect Nazi economics?   [9]

Glossary

Annex Acquire by force.

Boxer Rebellion An anti-foreign, anti-Christian revolt in China that was eventually joined by government soldiers with support from the Qing Dynasty. The revolt was put down by foreign troops.

Cabinet Ministers of a government.

Capital ships Large ships such as battleships and heavy cruisers.

Chancellor A position equivalent to prime minister in most countries and the most powerful official in Germany.

Coalition A government that includes multiple parties, often formed during times of national crisis.

Collectivization The Soviet Union's policy of ending privately owned and operated farms by consolidating farmers, farm animals and equipment in state-managed farms.

Conscription Required military service by a government for a specific length of time and usually for men only.

Coup d'état An overthrow of a state's government by individuals within that state.

Deficit spending When a government spends more money than it brings in through taxation, usually to stimulate a country's economy.

Diet Japan's legislature consisting of two houses, House of Representatives and House of Councillors, with the power to pass laws.

Embargo A restriction on the import of specific items or from a specific country.

Enabling Act Officially the 'Gesetz zur Behebung der Not von Volk und Reich' or 'Law to Remedy the Distress of the People and the State', this act allowed the government to rule by decree instead of through Parliament, including the implementation of laws that contradicted Germany's constitution.

Fascism A term derived from the Fascist Party of Italy. It refers to a governing philosophy that glorifies the state, war and sacrificing oneself for the state while de-emphasizing individual rights and freedoms. This term is often used to refer to non-democratic, militaristic governments.

Fascists Originally referring to Italy's ultranationalist Fascist Party, the term was eventually used to refer to most ultranationalist groups who advocated an end to or severe modification of republican forms of government in favour of authoritarian, nationalist single-party states.

Feudalism Form of government in which nobility and their associates, such as warriors, hold substantial governing power.

Great Depression A worldwide economic depression that led to massive unemployment, political instability, hunger and poverty, among other issues, starting from late 1929 and ending by the early 1940s, depending on the country or region.

Great Powers In this period, primarily European states such as Britain, France, Germany and Russia, but sometimes meant to include the USA, the Austro-Hungarian Empire and Italy.

Gross national product (GNP) The value of all goods and services produced by the citizens of a state over one year.

Guerrilla attacks Military attacks by small groups, usually on a larger military force.

Imperial preference A system of commerce created by lowering import taxes between areas of an empire, while increasing taxes on imports from countries outside the empire.

Indemnity A financial penalty.

International Settlement Area of Shanghai controlled by foreign governments where foreign-owned factories and other enterprises were located, and where many non-Chinese lived.

Kuomintang China's main political group, also known as the Guomindang, or Nationalists.

Kwantung Army Japan's most elite military unit before the Second World War, stationed in the Liaodong Peninsula, next to Manchuria.

League of Nations International organization that agreed to resolve international crises through diplomacy and not war that also established groups to address health issues, refugees, workers' rights and more.

Lebensraum German for living space, loosely defined as parts of eastern Europe.

Locarno treaties A series of agreements negotiated in 1925 at Locarno, Switzerland, between Britain, France, Germany, Italy and Belgium that secured Germany's western borders according to the terms of the Treaty of Versailles and measures to guarantee peace in Europe.

Mandates Lands formerly held by Germany and the Ottoman Empire that were to be administered by Britain, France, Belgium, Australia, New Zealand and Japan after the First World War for the League of Nations.

Meiji Constitution Japan's governing constitution from 1889 to 1947 that established a constitutional monarchy and defined the powers of the branches of Japan's government.

Meiji Emperor Emperor of Japan between 1867 and 1912 in whose name modernizing reforms were instituted.

Meiji Restoration The creation of a new government of Japan after centuries of military government, in which Japan's Emperor held new powers and new, more modern systems of governance were created; it is named after the ruling emperor of that period.

Monarchy A government led by a king or queen.

Monopolies Companies that control entire sections of the economy, such as steel production or shipbuilding.

National Socialists Abbreviated name for the National Socialist German Workers' Party or Nazi Party, an ultranationalist group.

Nazi–Soviet Pact More correctly known as the Molotov–Ribbentrop Pact. Germany and the Soviet Union agreed that neither country would attack the other or help other states attack the other. Additionally, there were economic aspects and secret sections that divided parts of central and eastern Europe into Soviet and German spheres of influence.

Neutrality Acts A series of US government laws that generally imposed embargoes on the sale of weapons to states at war.

Open Door Policy Policy advocated by the USA that called for all nations to have equal access to China's markets.

Ottoman Empire Empire that once covered most of the Middle East, much of north Africa and the Balkan peninsula of Europe, with its capital at Istanbul.

Pact of Steel More formally known as the 'Pact of Friendship and Alliance between Germany and Italy', the Pact publicly stated that the two countries supported and trusted each other; secret clauses stated that there would be a union of economic and military policies, although these were never enacted.

Pan-Germanism An idea from the early nineteenth century that all German-language speakers should live in the same country.

Plebiscite A national vote or referendum about one particular issue.

Privy Council Small government body of elites whose approval was required for laws, major political appointees and more; they controlled access to the Emperor of Japan and were heavily relied on by the Emperor owing to their prestige and experience.

Purges The removal of people, through loss of work, imprisonment or execution, who were deemed a threat by Soviet government authorities.

Qing Dynasty of China The ethnic Manchu family of rulers of China from 1644 to 1911.

Radical nationalism An extreme form of nationalism which can include racism and other forms of discrimination and prejudice against those not part of the nation, which is usually narrowly defined; this belief often justifies violence to achieve certain goals.

Rapallo Treaty Treaty signed in 1922 by the Soviet Union and Germany in which each renounced all claims against the other, recognized the other diplomatically and agreed to cooperate economically.

Reichstag Germany's Parliament.

Republic Form of government consisting of elected representatives of voters.

Rome–Berlin Axis Treaty of friendship between Germany and Italy in 1936, signalling an end to diplomatic cooperation between Italy and Britain and France.

Satellite state A state that is closely associated with another and is unable to act independently in many areas such as in economic or foreign policies.

Semi-isolation A policy of having limited involvement in international diplomacy.

Shidehara Diplomacy Japan's liberal foreign policy of the 1920s that sought to maintain good relations with Great Britain and the USA and a less aggressive policy towards China, named after Foreign Minister Kijūrō Shidehara.

Shōgun Hereditary military governors of Japan from 1192 to 1867.

Shōwa Emperor Grandson of the Meiji Emperor and often called by his personal name, Hirohito, outside Japan. He was preceded by the short reign of his mentally ill father, the Taishō Emperor.

Socialists People who believe that society should be as equal as possible financially and in terms of political rights.

Sphere of influence A territorial area where one nation has political and economic influence.

SS An acronym for *Schutzstaffel*, a Nazi paramilitary group that later functioned as the state police and operated a large part of the German economy.

Stimson Doctrine This policy stated that the USA would not recognize international border changes that resulted from war.

Sudeten German Party A German political party in Czechoslovakia in the 1930s that was closely allied to and adopted many of the ideals of the Nazi Party of Germany.

Suez Canal Major canal linking the Mediterranean and Red Seas and therefore the Atlantic and Indian Oceans.

Suffrage The right to vote.

Tōseiha The control faction of the Imperial Japanese Army active in the 1920s and the 1930s.

Total war A war with little or no restrictions on the nature of combat that requires combatant nations to mobilize all of the country's resources.

Trade barriers Means of restricting trade with other countries, usually by placing high taxes on foreign imports so that domestic goods can be sold more cheaply.

Treaty of Versailles Treaty imposed on Germany in 1919 by the victors of the First World War, which included financial penalties, severe military reductions and loss of land.

Tributary A state which presents gifts or funds to a stronger state for protection and/or as a sign of loyalty, respect and subservience.

Tripartite Pact An alliance involving initially Germany, Italy and Japan, coming into effect in September 1940 and eventually joined by Hungary, Romania, Slovakia, Bulgaria and Independent Croatia.

Ultranationalist A belief in which a person or state's nationality is considered superior to that of all others and usually involves racist and discriminatory beliefs against others not of the same nationality.

Vichy Government The common label for the southern part of France that was not occupied by German troops between 1940 and 1942, with its administrative centre in the town of Vichy. While it was allowed a certain degree of autonomy over its internal affairs, and allowed to oversee France's colonial empire, it had no meaningful independence from German authorities.

Wall Street Crash A rapid decline of the US stock market, located on Wall Street in New York city, in October 1929, which led to an economic crisis throughout the world.

World Disarmament Conference Conference held by the League of Nations which began in 1932, the aim of which was to reduce military sizes and weapons as a way to prevent future war.

Key figures

Brüning, Heinrich (1885–1970) Chancellor of Germany from 1930 to 1932.

Chamberlain, Neville (1869–1940) Prime Minister of Great Britain from 1937 to 1940.

Chiang Kai-shek (1887–1975) Leading military and political ruler of China after 1925, dominating the Kuomintang political party.

Daladier, Édouard (1884–1970) Prime Minister of France from 1938 to 1940.

Haile Selassie (1892–1975) Emperor of Abyssinia from 1930 to 1974.

Henlein, Konrad (1898–1945) Head of the Sudeten German Party during the Sudeten Crisis.

Hoare, Samuel (1880–1959) Britain's Secretary of State for Foreign Affairs in 1935.

Hull, Cordell (1871–1955) US Secretary of State from 1933 to 1944.

Laval, Pierre (1883–1945) Prime Minister and Foreign Minister in France in the 1930s.

Meiji Emperor Emperor of Japan between 1867 and 1912 in whose name modernizing reforms were instituted.

Roosevelt, Franklin D. (1882–1945) President of the USA from 1933 to 1945.

Seyss-Inquart, Arthur (1892–1946) Austrian Nazi politician who was Chancellor of Austria at the time of the *Anschluss* in 1938.

Shidehara, Kijūrō (1872–1951) Japan's Foreign Minister from 1924 to 1927 and from 1929 to 1931.

Shōwa Emperor Grandson of the Meiji Emperor and often called by his personal name, Hirohito, outside Japan. He was preceded by the short reign of his mentally ill father, the Taishō Emperor.

Stalin, Joseph (1878–1953) Authoritarian leader of the Soviet Union by the late 1920s.

von Hindenburg, Paul (1847–1934) A highly decorated general and President of Germany from 1925 to 1934.

Timeline

Japanese expansion in Asia 1931–41

1889	Meiji Constitution declared
1894	Japan occupied Korea
1894–5	First Sino-Japanese War
1895	Tripartite Intervention by Russia, Germany, France
1902	Anglo-Japanese Alliance
1904–5	Russo-Japanese War; Japan took control of South Manchurian Railway
1914–18	First World War; Japan took Shantung Peninsula; Japanese economy grew rapidly
1919–23	Japan's economy constricted, causing hardship for farmers and workers
1921–2	Washington Naval Conference and treaties limited Japanese navy
1923–7	Economic revival through rebuilding Tokyo earthquake damage
1925	Peace Protection Law allowed for the arrest of communists and others who advocated government changes
1927	Bank failures, economy rapidly constricted
1928	Army faction assassinated warlord ruler of Manchuria; acted against government policy
1929	Great Depression constricted economy further
1930	London Naval Conference, limited Japanese navy
1931	Mar: Attempted coup against government by military
	Sept: Mukden Incident; invasion of Manchuria by Japan
	Oct: Failed coup against government by military
	Dec: Lytton Commission formed to investigate Manchurian Crisis for League of Nations
1932	May: Failed coup against government by military
	Oct: Lytton Commission recommended Japan withdraw from Manchurian conquests
1933	Feb: League of Nations condemned Japan as an aggressor state
	Mar: Japan left League of Nations; Chinese province of Jehol captured by Japan
	May: Tanggu Truce signed with China recognizing Japanese conquests
1935	June: Umezu–He Agreement demilitarized much of northern China, removing Chinese armies; Mengjiang or Mengkukuo formed by Japan
1936	Feb: Military faction attempted to seize Emperor and overthrow government; coup failed
	Dec: Second United Front formed between Chinese factions to oppose Japan
1937–45	Aug 1937–Aug 1945: Second Sino-Japanese War
1938	July: Soviet–Japanese fighting along Manchukuo border
1939	May: Soviet–Japanese fighting in Mongolia; Soviets took territory to end fighting
1940	Sep: Japan began occupation of parts of French Indochina; USA halted sale of scrap iron and steel to Japan
1941	Jan: Second United Front in China collapsed
	July: All French Indochina occupied; USA halted sale of oil, seized Japanese assets in the USA
	Nov: US Hull Note demanded Japan withdraw from China and Indochina as well as Manchuria
	Dec: Japan attacked the USA at Pearl Harbor and other locations across Pacific Ocean region; British also attacked; USA declared war

Italian and German expansion 1933–40

1922	Mussolini became Prime Minister of Italy
1928	Soviet Union began mass industrialization in Five Year Plan, renewed this in 1932
1929	Oct: Great Depression began
1932	German unemployment at 26%
1933	Jan: Hitler became Chancellor of Germany
	Mar: *Gleichschaltung* began
	Oct: Germany left the League of Nations
1933	Mussolini became Minister of War, Air, Navy, Interior and Foreign Affairs as well as Prime Minister
1934	Jan: Polish–German Non-Aggression Pact signed
	July: German attempted to annex Austria but prevented by Italy
1934	New Plan for Germany's economy initiated; Soviet Union joined League of Nations
1935	Jan: Saar Plebiscite held
	Mar: Germany announced rearmament
	Apr: Stresa Front formed to ensure Germany's diplomatic isolation
	May: Franco-Soviet Treaty of Mutual Assistance
	June: Anglo-German Naval Treaty
	Oct: Italy invaded Abyssinia; League of Nations imposed economic sanctions on Italy
1936–9	Spanish Civil War; Italy committed troops and weapons to help Nationalists
1936	Mar: Germany remilitarized the Rhineland
	May: Italy left the League of Nations
	Sept: Four Year Plan for Germany's economy announced
	Oct: Rome–Berlin Axis announced
	Nov: Anti-Comintern Pact agreed by Germany and Japan

1938	Mar: Germany annexed Austria, confirmed by April plebiscite
	Sept: Munich Agreement granted the Sudeten areas of Czechoslovakia to Germany
	Oct: Poland seized part of Czechoslovakia; Slovakia granted autonomy; Germany requested negotiations for the return of Danzig
	Nov: Hungary seized large areas of Czechoslovakia, mostly from autonomous Slovakia
1939	Feb: Britain announced military alliance with France
	Mar: Rump of Czechoslovakia occupied by Germany; Slovakia made independent; Memel returned to Germany from Lithuania; Britain pledged to defend Poland's borders
	Apr: Italy invaded and annexed Albania
	May: Pact of Steel alliance signed by Italy and Germany
	23 Aug: Nazi–Soviet Pact announced
	25 Aug: Britain and Poland signed formal military alliance; Italy released from Pact of Steel obligations
	1 Sept: Germany invaded Poland
	3 Sept: Britain and France declared war on Germany

Answers

Case Study 1: Japanese expansion in Asia 1931–41

1 Causes of expansion

Page 7, Identifying relevant content

1 To maximize the power of the government and minimize the power of the Japanese people and by extension democracy.

2 They served as advisors to the government and worked to manage the entire government system.

3 'To pull the strings' means to control actions, indicating that Privy Council members had a great amount of power and influence on political decision making in Japan.

Page 9, Examining origin of a source

4 Nobuya Bamba is a professor of history, who specializes in the diplomatic and intellectual history of Japan. He is an expert on these topics, who possesses a broad and deep understanding of Japan's diplomatic and intellectual history.

5 Sources published after the events examined in the source have several advantages: the ability to understand the historical context, including causes and effects; can use a wide range of sources; and can consider multiple perspectives of a topic.

6 The University of British Columbia Press is associated with a university, meaning that it specializes in academic works and publishes material after careful examination of the value of the source to the field of study, giving its publications a great deal of credibility.

7 Because the scope of the book focuses on a period of history after the main topic of the excerpt, it might indicate that less attention and exploration in depth of the Tripartite Intervention was given than if the entire book had been focused on the Tripartite Intervention.

Page 9, Examining content of a source

8 The sources identifies ideas that influenced Japanese militarism and foreign policy such as national humiliation from the unequal treaties and the Tripartite Intervention. It also identifies 'Gashin shōtan' as influencing Japan's foreign policy goals. It also states that the Russo-Japanese War was fought to achieve the goal 'Gashin shōtan'.

9 The content is limited in the time period it covers, focusing primarily on the period around the Tripartite Intervention and the Russo-Japanese War, but does not address the entire time period of Meiji Japan.

Page 11, Identifying relevant content from an illustration

10 The use of a giant Cossack shows that Russia believed its military was a world power that could easily defeat the much smaller and less powerful Japanese military.

11 The text indicates that Russia could easily eat the Japanese figure whose skin would tear against the Cossack's teeth. This means the Russians believed that a war with Japan would be an easy victory. Because the Japanese figure would be breakfast, it also indicates that any war with Japan would be a quick victory.

12 The size and power of the Cossack illustrates the racial superiority of Russians. The small Japanese figure, whose face looks a little like a monkey, indicates that Russians believed the Japanese were racially inferior. A war between Russian and Japan would be a quick, easy victory for Russia.

Page 15, Examining a source's purpose

13 Autobiographies are written by someone who wants to tell their life story and to have their story published for a public audience.

14 By its nature, an autobiography can be influenced by personal biases. Those matters a person was particularly active in, interested in and helped create often get emphasized. Because the intended audience is public, there is the possibility that the author wants to create a positive impression of their actions and decisions.

15 By its nature, an autobiography can be influenced by personal biases. Those matters a person was not active in, interested in or played a role in might be ignored or given little attention in the autobiography. Because the intended audience is public, there is the possibility that the author might ignore matters that were embarrassing or regrettable. It also is possible that such matters were mentioned but with minimal and or partial details.

■ Page 15, Connecting purpose to content

16 He was trying to gain political support for his goal of rapprochement with China as part of Shidehara Diplomacy.

17 Shidehara wanted to persuade the Diet to support his policy. Therefore, the contents of the statement would be designed to give the best impression of his policy. He would be likely to de-emphasize or ignore information that could give a negative impression to Diet members.

18 Varies by student.

■ Page 21, Summarizing a source

19 The Japanese government was concerned that Chang's presence in north China would lead to conflict with Chiang Kai-shek that would threaten Japanese interests in Manchuria.

20 The Japanese government believed that they could cooperate and co-exist with Chang's army in Manchuria.

21 The Kwantung Army wanted to make Japan's influence in Manchuria impregnable.

22 The events regarding Chang and Manchuria indicate growing tensions between the Japanese government and radical factions in the military.

■ 2 Japan's expansion and the international response

■ Page 31, Identifying significant knowledge

1	Knowledge statement	Significant	Not significant
	An explosion occurred on 18 September 1931		✗
	Japanese troops had been stationed in Manchuria since 1905		✗
	Japanese troops moved swiftly to defend Japanese interests	✗	
	Japan's leaders declared Chinese troops responsible	✗	
	Damage to the railway was light		✗
	The incident was part of a wider plan to extend Japanese power in Manchuria	✗	

■ Page 31, Marking an evaluation of a source

2 1/4. The response partially identifies the origin of the source, but lacks details on the name of the author, title of the book and when it was published. However, it does identify it as a history book, showing limited understanding about origin. There is no reference to the purpose of the source. No credit can be given for purpose. Limited content is identified – only the Manchurian Crisis, but no other details. The response makes one connection between value and content, but makes no connections between origin or purpose. The response on limitations has no relevance to the context of 'a historian studying Japanese expansion and the international response on Japan's road to war'. No connections are made between limitation and origin, purpose or content. Limited understanding of the evaluation of a source is shown.

■ Page 33, Analysing a political cartoon

3 A doormat is something people step on and walkover before entering a building. It also is used to describe a submissive person. Therefore, the symbolism shows the League of Nations as submissive and incapable of enforcing its covenant against Japan for its actions in Manchuria.

4 The action of the British Foreign Secretary kneeling on the ground and applying make-up on the women who represents the League of Nations is exaggeration because such a person would never kneel on the ground to apply make-up.

5 The label 'face-saving outfit' explains the purpose of the make-up on the League of Nations. Doing something face saving means to do something because it is important to look like proper action is taking place, but that real effort is not made.

6 The actions of the League of Nations in the Manchurian Crisis were not designed to stop Japan in Manchuria. They were designed to show that the League of Nations tried to do something, but knew it probably could not make any impact. They also show that the British Foreign Secretary was influential in shaping the League's actions and that Britain was not committed to taking serious action in Manchuria.

■ Page 35, Writing a compare and contrast response

7 Some possible responses include the following. These are suggested responses, but do not represent all possible responses to the question.

Comparing:

- Source C states that small countries could lose part of their territory to accommodate larger countries. Similarly, Source D states that China reconciled itself to the loss of a province to Japan.
- Source C claims that Japan profited from being a Great Power and Source D states that Japan was not condemned by the League of Nations.
- Both Source C and Source D make reference to problems the League of Nations would have in Abyssinia.

Contrasting:

- Source C asserts that the League of Nations and collective security were permanently damaged by the Manchurian Crisis. However, Source D claims that the League of Nations grew stronger.
- Source D claims that Britain played a positive role in improving the League of Nations, whereas Source C states that all Great Powers used the League of Nations to their own benefit.
- Source C focuses on how the Great Powers preyed upon smaller nations. Source D, however, states that Japan, a Great Power, was condemned by the League of Nations.

■ Page 37, Examining origin of a source

8 The author of the excerpt is Japan's Prime Minister Kanoe. The description identifies the excerpt as a section of a speech by Kanoe. This signifies that Kanoe gave the speech to Japan's Diet in 1937. Kanoe's speech is included in the book *Modern Japan: A History of Documents*. The title of this book informs us that it is a collection of historical sources about modern Japan. Therefore, James L. Huffman is the historian who collected and edited all the documents in the book, including the speech used in Source E. He is not the author of the speech.

9 The source is a speech given by Japan's prime minister to Japan's Diet. Speeches made by a head of government, like a prime minister, have several purposes: to

- state a government's official position on a particular development
- justify a government's official position on a particular development
- identify goals and aims of a government
- persuade an audience to support an official position, goal, aim, piece of legislation, and so on.

In this speech, Prime Minister Kanoe is both stating and justifying his government's official position on the Marco Polo Bridge Incident and Japan's response to the incident.

10 Because Japan will respond with force to the Marco Polo Bridge Incident, Prime Minister Kanoe portrays China as the cause of incident and Japan's need to use force. Words Kanoe uses to create this portrait include:

- 'failed to understand the true motive'
- 'aroused a spirit of contempt'
- 'outburst of uncontrolled national sentiment, the situation has fast been aggravated, spreading in scope'.

In contrast, Japan is portrayed as 'patient to the utmost' and 'forced to deal a firm and decisive blow.' Kanoe justifies Japan as reasonable and uses force as a last resort because of China's actions.

■ Page 39, Spot the mistake

11 The answer does not provide all of the important information on origin. It omits the date and the title of the article. The purpose is well written. The weakest part of the answer is the reply on value. Being a primary source does not make it valuable. All sources have value and limitations based on what is being studied or examined. In this example, value results from Taylor's expertise in oriental studies. Value also comes from it being a contemporary evaluation of Japan's military in China that may reflect American attitudes about Japan's military capability during the time leading up to war. Simply stating that an author has a bias shows minimal understanding of how biases affect the value or limitation of a source. It would have been better to explain Taylor's potential bias in the context of increasing tensions between the USA and Japan in 1940, as well as the role of racism in shaping biases. More would be required for full marks, however. The source is limited because its content focuses only on Japan's military in China. It does not address other factors in Japan's expansion and the international response.

■ Page 43, Summarizing a source

12 Materials and supplies used by Chinese forces against Japan in the Second Sino-Japanese War passed over the border from French Indochina.

13 Japan used diplomacy in an attempt to get France to recognize that Japan was in a state of war with China and Japan's belligerent rights. Japan considered bombing the Yunnan railway in an attempt to force a diplomatic solution.

14 In the autumn of 1939, France went to war with Germany at the start of the Second World War in Europe.

■ Case study 2: Italian and German expansion 1933–40

■ 3 Interwar conditions in Europe and Italian foreign policy 1933–6

■ Page 55, Identifying relevant content

1 'High protective tariff' and 'imperial preference'.

2 The first sentence describes a warning about 'high protective tariff' and 'imperial preference', indicating that 'high protective tariff' and 'imperial preference' would have some type of negative effect. Recognizing their effect identifies important, relevant knowledge.

3 High protective tariff and imperial preference would increase Britain's isolation from the Continent and decrease its political influence on countries on the Continent.

4 'Urged the importance of' and 'which might otherwise'.

5 The phrase 'urged the importance of' identifies something significant. The phrase 'which might otherwise' identifies what will happen if the important recommendation was not implemented.

6 It was important for Britain to provide a market for the Baltic states and Poland. If Britain did not provide them a market, Nazi Germany (Berlin) or communist Soviet Union (Moscow) would provide the market and benefit from it.

7 'It was argued' and 'to prevent them'.

8 The phrase 'it was argued' references an argument. An argument, in this case, means a reasoned judgement about some matter in order to persuade. The point being argued is important, relevant knowledge. The phrase 'to prevent them' indicates what would happen if the recommendation made in the argument was not implemented.

9 It was important for Britain to buy cereal and grain from Hungary and Yugoslavia (the point argued). If Britain did buy cereal and grain from them (Hungary and Yugoslavia), Germany's market would become more important to them and increase Germany's economic influence on Hungary and Yugoslavia (which should be prevented).

■ Page 55, Identifying relevant content from a table

10 Wholesalers buy products in large quantities from manufacturers. If they receive less money for the products they bought, they will have less money to buy products from manufacturers. Therefore, there is less demand for manufactured products and manufacturers must reduce the amount they produce. With fewer goods being manufactured, fewer workers are needed in factories.

11 Estimated percentage of unemployed workers by 1933 and percentage change in industrial production.

12 Decreased exports resulted in decreased sales of products and goods to foreign countries, which meant decreased revenue for industry. Decreased revenue led to a decreased demand for products and goods. This led to a decreased need for workers. This effect increased unemployment. The impact of this cause and effect cycle could be minimized if a country could increase domestic sales of goods or products or find a substitute market for its exports.

13 Britain's use of imperial preference meant it had a substitute market for its exports. This answer is an example of connecting statistics from a table to knowledge and understanding of topics. It also is an example of using own knowledge in connection with source knowledge, which is important when answering question 12 in the Paper 1 exam.

■ Page 57, Examining origin of a source

14 Bruno Heilig is the author of Source C. Do not be confused and believe it was Arthur Madsen. The title of the source is the first piece of information given. The use of quotation marks indicates the title of an article or essay. Bruno Heilig is identified as the author of the essay with the use of the preposition by. The words in italics indicate the title of a book. In this case it indicates the book in which the essay was published. The book is a collection of essays related to the topic of the title. Arthur Madsen is identified as the editor of the book. As editor, Madsen collected appropriate essays to include in the book, as well as editing essays as necessary and writing any text needed to fully develop the topic and place the essays into a proper context.

15 Journalists learn and study the events they report on as they happen. To better explain, it means that journalists often consider events and actions from the past, usually the recent past, to provide the context to the events they report. Therefore, Heilig would have some expertise on the political situation in Germany that he wrote about.

16 Journalists are more focused on reporting current events. Even though they may do some historical study to help understand context, they do not study the past in the depth or with the analytical skills of historians. This limits the journalists' ability to understand the full historical context of the events they report. Also, writings of journalists are contemporary to the events they report. Therefore, they do not have the ability to perceive events from many years in the future. Many historical forces and connections cannot be seen until many years have passed, allowing for more sources to be uncovered and for a deeper understanding of the historical context of the times in which events happened.

■ Page 57, Identifying significant knowledge

17

Knowledge statement	Significant	Not significant
Was there a link between the economic and the political collapse? Eventually, yes	✗	
For as unemployment grew, and with it poverty and the fear of poverty, so grew the influence of the Nazi Party	✗	
The representation of the middle class practically speaking disappeared	✗	
In January 1933, Hitler was appointed *Reichskanzler* [Chancellor]; he attained power, as I said before, quite legally	✗	

■ Page 59, Identifying relevant content from an illustration

18 The use of a brick wall marking the borders of Germany suggests that the two regions of Germany were forcibly separated by an unnatural barrier for the creation of Polish territory. The fence surrounding the Free City of Danzig suggests that the residents of Danzig were not actually free but prisoners of the terms of the Treaty of Versailles and forcibly separated from their German homeland.

19 The route lines show how Germany and the region of eastern Germany were connected into one continuous country. The Germans living in the eastern region were isolated from their homeland because the brick walls broke the transportation lines that connected them to their homeland. Because brick walls can be dismantled, the illustration suggests that Germans had the right to once again be united by these transportation routes.

■ Page 61, Examining a source's purpose

20 As Mussolini mentioned in his speech, he wanted to establish man's nature as warlike. Therefore, war is a natural state of existence and not something to be avoided. Because it was a speech by the leader of Italy, the speech desired to establish a justification for Italy's foreign policy goals.

21 Both Lamont's biographical details and the title of the book suggest he intended his book to persuade his audience of the positive characteristics of socialism.

22 As a socialist, Lamont almost certainly opposed fascism. His ideological perspective may affect the sources he used in his book designed to persuade opinions about socialism. In this case, it meant he selected a speech that made Mussolini appear like a warmonger. However, the words were uttered by Mussolini in this speech. While Lamont's socialism might lead him to including mostly negative evidence about fascism, using a direct quote from Mussolini does not change Mussolini's purpose nor the idea he wanted to promote in his speech.

■ Page 63, Writing a compare and contrast response

	Similarities		Differences	
	Source H	**Source I**	**Source H**	**Source I**
Content knowledge	• Invasion of Italy • Government provided war-related commissions to industry • One method of sacrificing for Italy can be seen in mobilization, which required Italians to serve in the military regardless of their preference to do so or not	• Expansion of the nations • Empire demands discipline and the co-ordination of all forces • Calls for individuals to respond to the call of duty and offer to sacrifice themselves for Italy	• Specifies economic benefits resulting from co-ordinated war efforts	• Makes reference to general benefits to Italy, but provides no specific examples
Argument			• Makes an argument about the cause and effect relationship between Italy's economy and preparations for war	• Makes a doctrinal argument about the benefits of fascism in general
Perspective			• Provides a historical perspective on Italy's expansion	• Mussolini's fascist perspective

23 Using the chart above, connect the bullet points recorded in row. Each pair of bullet points can be used to replace the ellipses from the suggested sentence structures in the text box above.

■ Page 67, Summarizing a source

24 Both Britain and France were reluctant to use force, either military or economic.

25 No country was willing to intervene in a forcible manner against Italy.

26 Mussolini had too much political interest invested in Abyssinia and would have gone to war with any power that intervened there unless he faced a force of overwhelming power.

27 No country had the political will to use force against Mussolini, who would have waged war against any country that did intervene.

■ Page 71, Summarizing a source

28 Because Italy was not ready for war, either militarily or economically, Mussolini worked to delay Italy's commitment to Germany to support them in times of war.

■ 4 German foreign policy 1933–40

■ Page 81, Identifying relevant content

1 The amount of German imports could not exceed the amount of revenue generated by German exports. In addition, imports needed licences based on Germany's needs.

2 Imports were most likely to be essential items such as raw materials and food.

■ Page 81, Identifying relevant content from an illustration

3 The use of sarcasm with the phrase 'Hurrah, the butter is all gone' indicates dissatisfaction with the government. Combined with the context of Goering's speech about ore being necessary for strength while food makes people fat, the captions show disapproval for economic policies that emphasized military production while reducing spending for food.

4 The use of metal tools as food shows that consumer goods like food are sacrificed because the government invested heavily in industrial production. The image of the baby biting the edge of a Nazi axe suggests that Nazi economic policies are dangerous to the populace.

■ Page 83, Identifying significant knowledge

5

Knowledge statement	Significant	Not significant
The armed forces themselves were anxious to rebuild German military power cautiously, step-by-step, so that they could control its pace and character themselves	✗	
Infrastructure of military life – barracks, airfields, training schools – that had been shut down or destroyed during the period of enforced disarmament		✗ The condition of being shut down explains why Germany had to rebuild, but is not as significant in regard to Germany's rearmament policies. It is mostly background information
The first air force production programmes were largely devoted to building trainer aircraft	✗	
Tank production was slow to get going and the programme for naval shipbuilding laid down in 1934 had achieved little before the late 1930s		✗ This statement provides evidence that supports the overarching statement below it
Remilitarization on any scale took time to achieve because Germany began in 1933 from a very low base	✗	
The armed forces themselves were anxious to rebuild German military power cautiously, step-by-step, so that they could control its pace and character themselves	✗	

■ Page 85, Examining origin of a source and purpose

6 Because a memo is for internal communication, there is no need for the author to adjust content in regard to how an outside audience might react to it. As a formal means of communication, the author probably carefully considered what content to include in it, especially with consideration to who receives the memo. In this case, von Bülow can make reference to negative information without worrying about public opinion.

7 Von Bülow was giving Hitler his expert analysis on German rearmament in relation to France's military.

8 Von Bülow was a state secretary with expertise in foreign affairs. He would have had a strong understanding of Germany and its relations to foreign powers.

■ Page 85, Examining content of a source

9 Simon believes Britain should recognize German rights to act in accordance with protocols reserved for any nation with legitimate concerns, including making agreements with Germany regarding rearmament. He argues that treating Germany as a nation with legitimate concerns and rights would lead to greater stability in Europe.

10 Simon's argument reflects a general understanding of Britain's foreign policy towards Germany during the early to mid-1930s. Given its date of February 1935, it illustrates thinking in Britain that led to the Anglo-German Naval Treaty in June 1935.

11 As a primary source written in February 1935, it cannot reflect developments in German foreign policy or international relations after that date. The perspective of the source is British. It might suggest developments that German foreign policy reacted to, but it does not give great insight into the German perspective of its foreign policy. Nor does it provide perspective of any other country on German foreign policy from 1933 to 1940.

■ Page 89, Identifying relevant content from an illustration

12 The presence of significant Nazi symbols suggests that Austria is already part of Germany and voting in support of the plebiscite is only a formality to the natural state of affairs.

13 The concept that people of the same blood belong to one empire reinforces the belief that Austria should be part of the German empire because Austrians have German blood. It illustrates an effective argument to support the *Anschluss*.

■ Page 91, Writing a compare and contrast response

14 Some possible responses include the following. These are suggested responses, but do not represent all possible responses to the question.

Comparing:

● Both Source I and Source J show Hitler's appeals to diplomacy in the Sudeten Crisis matter.
● In Source I, Hitler makes reference to the diplomatic tensions between Czechoslovakia and Germany, which is similar to the proposed strategy of using diplomatic tensions in the crisis specified in Source J.
● Source J shows how Germany is a threat to Czechoslovakia and in Source I Hitler claims that if Germany's demands are not met it would threaten war between Germany and Czechoslovakia.

Contrasting:

● Source I asserts that Germany has no interest in seizing all of Czechoslovakia, whereas Source J shows that German conquest of Czechoslovakia was Germany's intention.
● Hitler praises and thanks Britain's Prime Minister Chamberlain for his peace efforts because Germany wanted peace; however, Source J reveals that Germany's diplomatic efforts at peace were not genuine, but that Germany had been planning an invasion of Czechoslovakia for many months.
● Source I contains a claim that Germany's last territorial claim in Europe was the Sudetenland, but Source J indicates that Germany had more territorial ambitions.

■ Page 93, Summarizing a source

15 (1) The French Government and the German Government fully share the conviction that pacific and neighbourly relations between France and Germany constitute one of the essential elements of the consolidation of the situation in Europe and of the preservation of peace. Consequently <u>both Governments will endeavour [work] with all their might to assure the development of the relations between their countries in this direction.</u>

(2) <u>Both Governments</u> agree that no question of a territorial nature remains in suspense [unresolved] between their countries and <u>solemnly recognize as permanent the frontier between their countries as it is actually drawn.</u>

(3) <u>Both Governments are resolved</u>, without prejudice to their special relations with Third Powers, to remain in contact on all questions of importance to both their countries and <u>to have recourse to mutual consultation in case any complications arising out of these questions should threaten to lead to international difficulties.</u>

■ Page 95, Summarizing a source

16 The Soviets hoped to cause conflict between Germany and the West and to isolate Poland.

17 The Soviets wanted to draw the western powers [neutralize their effectiveness], isolate Poland and improve their negotiating position with Germany.

18 Both the Nazis and the west held assumptions that lessened their position in negotiations: the Nazi assumed western inaction and the west assumed Soviet cooperation.

Exam practice answers

■ 1 Causes of expansion, page 29

9 (a) Effects of the Great Depression on Japanese expansion could include:

- The military could take advantage of the lower levels of society for its expansionist wars.
- Economic difficulties from the Great Depression made expansionist policies attractive to businesses that hoped for new markets.
- Politicians promoted expansionist policies in order to appear strong to attract support.

Award 1 mark for each relevant point up to 3 marks.

(b) Messages could include:

- Japan already controlled parts of China and intended to expand its conquest of China.
- The size of the Japanese soldier indicates that Japan's military was so powerful it would be almost impossible to stop.

Award 1 mark for each relevant point up to 2 marks.

10 Possible relevant source analyses include:

- Origin: A newspaper article written by Jeff Kingston published in *The Japan Times*, 20 February 2016.
- Purpose: A commentary using the 26th February Incident to make a political comment about contemporary political issues in Japan.
- Content: A description of the 26th February Incident that includes analyses of its causes and effects.
- Value: The author is the Director of Asian Studies for Temple University Japan, indicating his expertise in Japanese history and modern Asia. The source is an insightful analysis of the influence of ultranationalism and militarism in Japan's politics in the 1930s. The source identifies several key factors that shaped political decisions and goals in Japan during the 1930s.
- Limitations: As a newspaper article, the source does not go into great depth. The article examines only one incident from 1936 of ultranationalism and militarism. It does not provide any knowledge or analyses on other factors before or after the 26th February Incident. Because the source was used to comment on a contemporary political event in Japan, its analyses may be influenced by its purpose to influence the audience on government policy.

For a maximum of 4 marks, candidates should refer to origin, purpose and content in their analysis of value and limitations.

11 Possible relevant comparison/contrast responses could include:

For compare:

- Both sources refer to the 26th February Incident.
- An aggressive Japanese military is the subject of both sources.
- Both sources recognize the military has concerns about a strong national defence policy.
- Both sources show that Japan's military was willing to interfere in domestic policies.

For contrast:

- Source L focuses on the perspective of the radicals in the military while Source K focuses on the perspective of the Emperor.
- Source K addresses the aftermath of the 26th February Incident, but Source L concentrates on the reasons for the incident.

- Source L identifies the concerns and justifications of young, radical officers, whereas Source K implies that the military in general, including some senior officers, possess extreme ideas.
- Source K states that the military has no right to influence economic policies, however, Source L shows that economic concerns were a main motivating factor for the military officers involved in the 26th February Incident.
- Source L indicates that the military wanted radical changes, in contrast to Source K that states explicitly that radical changes could not happen.

Do not demand all of the above. If only one source is discussed award a maximum of 2 marks. If the two sources are discussed separately award 3 marks or with excellent linkage 4–5 marks. For a maximum 6 marks expect a detailed running comparison/contrast.

12 Possible relevant essay material could include:

- Source I: The military could use ultranationalism to gain the support of the lower levels of society. Business leaders and politicians could use expansionist foreign policies to their advantage.
- Source J: The Japanese military intended to conquer China. The Japanese military may have been shaping Japan's policies in China.
- Source K: Japan's government needed to consider the demands of the military in making policy and keeping domestic stability. It also suggests that the influence of Japan's military on government decisions was increasing.
- Source L: Japan's military was willing to intervene in order to shape Japan's policies. In its most extreme form, this intervention included the use of violence to achieve goals. Some in the military believed Japan suffered from decay and corruption, requiring the military to restore Japan to its proper path.

Own knowledge could include evidence from:

- The Mukden Incident.
- The Manchurian Crisis.
- The Kwantung Army.
- Japan's withdrawal from the League of Nations.
- Political assassinations by military personnel.
- The Marco Polo Bridge Incident.
- The Second Sino-Japanese War 1937–45.
- The Nanjing Massacre.
- Japan's economy being dictated by military needs for fighting in China.
- Japan's alliances with Germany and Italy: the Anti-Comintern Pact, the Tripartite Pact and the Rome–Berlin–Tokyo Axis.
- Japan's invasion and occupation of French Indochina.
- Japan's attack on Pearl Harbor.
- Japan's attack on other Pacific territories of the USA, Britain and the Netherlands.

Do not expect all of the above and accept other relevant material. Response should be focused on the question. Clear references should be made to the sources, and these references should be used effectively as evidence to support the analysis. The response demonstrates accurate and relevant own knowledge. There should be effective synthesis of own knowledge and source material.

■ 2 Japan's expansion and the international response, page 53

9 (a) Possible reasons that led to Japan's military escalation in China include:

- Chiang joined the Second United Front.
- Chiang began fighting the Japanese Army.
- Japan reacted viscerally to stop what they saw as the increasing threat of communism.

Award 1 mark for each relevant point up to 3 marks.

(b) Messages could include:

- The creation of Manchukuo, as symbolized by the flag, brought peace to the region, as seen by the doves.
- Japan's rule in Manchukuo was peaceful and protected China's people.

Award 1 mark for each relevant point up to 2 marks.

10 Possible relevant source analyses include:

- Origin: A book, *The Struggle for North*, written by George E. Taylor, a professor of oriental studies at the University of Washington, USA, published by the Institute of Pacific Relations in 1940, New York, USA.
- Purpose: To provide an account of Japan's actions in China during the Second-Sino Japanese War for an audience of international relations specialists and academics based on the publisher.
- Content: A description of Japan's harsh treatment of China's peasants and why Chinese guerrillas fought Japan's army. It also details the defeat of the guerrillas and severe treatment of captured guerrillas, as well as the peasantry following the end of the fighting.
- Value: The author was a professor of oriental studies, making him an expert on Asian matters. His analysis is supported by his expertise. He probably had good contacts in China that provided him with evidence of Japan's action taken against the Chinese people. Therefore, it contained information from primary sources giving insight into events in China in the late 1930s.
- Limitations: The source is limited in scope. It refers to events specific to one area in China during a time period that covers only part of the demands of the question. Even though Taylor was an expert, his analysis was restricted by the limited amount of information he received about events in China. Unlike academic historical works, it does not benefit from a big picture understanding of events. Given the publication date of 1940, his perception of Japan may have been influenced by Japan's aggressive military policy.

For a maximum of 4 marks, candidates should refer to origin, purpose and content in their analysis of value and limitations.

11 Possible relevant comparison/contrast responses could include:

For compare:

- Both sources refer to China's resistance to Japan.
- Both sources indicate that Japan acted with military force against China.
- Both sources show China's people held Japan's army in contempt.
- Both sources show that Japan's military was willing to interfere in domestic policies.

For contrast:

- Source L claims that Japan sought a peaceful settlement to its presence in China, whereas Source K implies Japan used forceful methods from the beginning of its presence in China.
- Source K's perspective is anti-Japan, but Source L possesses a Japanese perspective.
- Source K classifies Japan's actions against China as terror; on the other hand, Source L explains that Japan's actions were a legitimate and justified use of force.
- Source L blames China for the violence; however, Source K blames Japan.

Do not demand all of the above. If only one source is discussed award a maximum of 2 marks. If the two sources are discussed separately award 3 marks or with excellent linkage 4–5 marks. For a maximum 6 marks expect a detailed running comparison/contrast.

12 Possible relevant essay material could include:

- Source I: The source gives evidence of Japan's militarism and its expansionist policies.
- Source J: Japan's policy towards Manchuria resulted in a peaceful new country, Manchukuo.
- Source K: Japan was willing to resort to war and terror to achieve its objectives in China. It suggest that the policy was one of conquest and oppression.
- Source L: Japan's policy was benevolent, desiring nothing more than cooperation between fellow Asian nations. China's misunderstanding of Japan's intentions required Japan to react with force.

Own knowledge could include evidence from:

- The Mukden Incident.
- The Manchurian Crisis.
- Manchukuo.
- The Umezu–He Agreement.
- The Marco Polo Bridge Incident.
- The Second Sino-Japanese War, 1937–45.
- The Nanjing Massacre.

- Japan's economy being dictated by military needs for fighting in China.
- Chinese Civil War.
- Mao Zedong.
- League of Nations.
- Lytton Commission.

Do not expect all of the above and accept other relevant material. Response should be focused on the question. Clear references should be made to the sources, and these references should be used effectively as evidence to support the analysis. The response demonstrates accurate and relevant own knowledge. There should be effective synthesis of own knowledge and source material.

■ 3 Interwar conditions in Europe and Italian foreign policy 1933–6, page 79

9 **(a)** Possible responses showing how Haile Selassie justified his call for assistance from the League of Nations include:

- Abyssinia was being attacked by a much stronger country.
- He had asked for previous assistance to allow Abyssinia to defend itself, but was refused.
- He referred to Article 16 and the idea of collective security to remind members of the League of Nations of their duty.

Award 1 mark for each relevant point up to 3 marks.

(b) Messages could include:

- Italy, as symbolized by Mussolini, violated international law by using poison gas to commit atrocities against the people of Abyssinia.
- Italy's atrocities were justified because of racist beliefs about Abyssinians.

Award 1 mark for each relevant point up to 2 marks.

10 Possible relevant source analyses include:

- Origin: A book, *The League of Nations: Its Life and Times, 1920–1946* written by F.S. Northedge, a professor of international relations at the London School of Economics, published by Holmes & Meier, New York, USA, in 1986.
- Purpose: To provide an academic examination of the history of the League of Nations that could be read by both academics and a general audience.
- Content: Britain and France had no real desire to use force against Italy over Abyssinia. Mussolini had no intention of stopping his conquest of Abyssinia. These are evidence of the cynicism of the major powers of the League of Nations.
- Value: The author is an expert on international relations, giving his interpretations about the League of Nations and international diplomacy authority. As an academic history text, it benefits from access to a wide variety of sources providing substantive evidence that heightens the effectiveness of the author's analyses. The content shows reasons for the weakness of the League of Nations and why acts of aggression were left unchallenged.
- Limitations: The source is limited in scope. Its main focus is the League of Nations, not Italy or Abyssinia. Therefore, it does not contain the breadth and depth of a historical text focused on the Abyssinian Crisis. It is limited also because it does not provide information on causes or effects or on the actions of Italy or Abyssinia. While Northedge is an expert in international relations, he does not have the same degree of expertise for examining political or military history.

For a maximum of 4 marks, candidates should refer to origin, purpose and content in their analysis of value and limitations.

11 Possible relevant comparison/contrast responses could include:

For compare:

- Both sources refer to reluctance by Britain and France to abide by the terms of Article 16 of the League of Nations.
- Both sources show there was no desire by Britain and France to place oil sanctions or an embargo against Italy.
- Both sources illustrate structural weaknesses of the League of Nations.

For contrast:

- Source L describes Britain's concern about Germany, whereas Source K makes no reference to Germany or its role in the crisis.
- Source K's perspective blames inaction by Britain and France, as well as Mussolini's aggression, but Source L includes Abyssinia and the League of Nations in the blame for the crisis.
- Source L examines dissension within Britain's government about its policy towards Italy and Germany; however, Source K refers only to Britain's reluctance to use force.

Do not demand all of the above. If only one source is discussed award a maximum of 2 marks. If the two sources are discussed separately award 3 marks or with excellent linkage 4–5 marks. For a maximum 6 marks expect a detailed running comparison/contrast.

12 Possible relevant essay material could include:

- Source I: Abyssinia needed support from the League of Nations to fight an aggressive Italy.
- Source J: Racism influenced Italy's foreign policy. Italy and Mussolini were willing to use terror and violence to achieve their goals.
- Source K: Mussolini wanted war with Abyssinia regardless of international condemnations or attempts at collective security. Britain and France were not committed to their League of Nations obligations. Also, they had no desire to use force against Italy.
- Source L: Structural problems within the League of Nations made it weak and ineffective. Britain was becoming more concerned with Germany and did not want to alienate Italy. Haile Selassie shared in the blame through his stubbornness and willingness to use the League of Nations to maintain his power.

Own knowledge could include evidence from:

- League of Nations weakened by the Manchurian Crisis and the withdrawal of Japan and Germany.
- Nationalism in Italy.
- Beliefs of fascism.
- Benito Mussolini.
- Rebirth of a Roman Empire.
- Great Depression made more aggressive foreign policy appealing in Italy and to Mussolini.
- The Wal-Wal Incident.

■ 4 German foreign policy 1933–40, page 107

9 (a) Possible responses of relative directives of the New Plan include:

- Imports must conform to Germany's needs.
- Imports could require a licence that would differentiate between essential and non-essential products.
- Imports should come only from countries willing to purchase German goods.

Award 1 mark for each relevant point up to 3 marks.

(b) Messages could include:

- The Nazis have had tremendous success stimulating Germany's economy and industrial production.
- A vote for the Nazis would maintain Germany's economic growth, but voting against them would risk economic repercussions from the Great Depression.

Award 1 mark for each relevant point up to 2 marks.

10 Possible relevant source analyses include:

- Origin: An excerpt from a book, *Nazi Conspiracy and Aggression*, Volume 1, published by Office of the United States Chief of Counsel for Prosecution of Axis Criminality in 1946.
- Purpose: To record the documentary evidence compiled by US and British prosecutors who tried Nazi leaders for war crimes at the International Military Tribunal in Nuremberg, Germany, that proved the guilt of those on trial.

- Content: The economic policy of Nazi Germany had a secret intent to militarize industry and prepare Germany for war from the earliest period of Nazi rule.
- Value: Value comes from the exhaustive research on German and Nazi documents, interviews and other pertinent government records conducted by Allied prosecution teams in the immediate aftermath of Germany's defeat in the Second World War. Prosecution teams consisted of highly skilled and successful legal minds in their respective countries, making them experts in the collection of evidence. Although the source covers a wide scope, the great breadth and depth of the collection of evidence makes this valuable even for a more narrow topic.
- Limitations: The aim of prosecutors is the show criminal guilt of defendants. The purpose affects the selection of evidence used to defend an argument. Much of the evidence collected focused on a specific perspective – alleged criminal activity. Perspectives and knowledge related to foreign policy, economic policy, economic outcomes and other such factors may not be considered from a larger perspective. Because the source is a primary source, it does not contain perspectives developed after the military trials.

For a maximum of 4 marks, candidates should refer to origin, purpose and content in their analysis of value and limitations.

11 Possible relevant comparison/contrast responses could include:

For compare:

- Both sources describe the desire to rebuild Germany's military.
- Both sources make reference to military concerns affecting economic policy.
- Source L identifies the role of the Nazi regime (Reich Defence Council and Minister of Economics) in shaping remilitarization, which is implied by the claim of the military, in Source K, to try to control the character of remilitarization.

For contrast:

- Source L presents a sense of urgency surrounding remilitarization, but Source K emphasizes that the military sought a cautious approach to it.
- Source K describes limited success of remilitarization, whereas Source L refers to a war economy where economic policies and concerns focus on military production, suggesting that Germany's army rapidly increased.
- Source K focuses on military concerns, unlike Source L which places significant emphasis on economic matters.
- Source L declares that remilitarization was driven by plans to go to war; however, Source K only concentrates on rebuilding the military with no mention of war.

Do not demand all of the above. If only one source is discussed award a maximum of 2 marks. If the two sources are discussed separately award 3 marks or with excellent linkage 4–5 marks. For a maximum 6 marks expect a detailed running comparison/contrast.

12 Possible relevant essay material could include:

- Source I: Schacht's New Plan was designed to shape foreign trade to benefit Germany's economy, not their foreign trading partners' economies.
- Source J: Germany's economy boomed because of Nazi economic policy. The poster uses nationalism to win votes for the Nazis in the coming election.
- Source K: Germany's remilitarization was a long-term process that took years to fully mature. It implies that the German military's desire for a cautious approach to remilitarization was the key influencing factor.
- Source L: The Nazi regime desired war from its earliest days in power and developed secret plans to militarize the economy in order to rebuild Germany's army. The primary economic factor in decision making was remilitarization.

Own knowledge could include evidence from:

- Four Year Plan and Hermann Goering.
- 'Guns or Butter'.
- Autarky.
- Synthetic oil and synthetic rubber.
- Nazism.
- *Lebensraum*.
- *Gleichschaltung*.
- Rapallo Treaty and the Polish–German Non-Aggression Pact.
- Anglo-German Naval Treaty.
- Treaty of Versailles.
- Remilitarization of the Rhineland.
- Sudeten Crisis and the Munich Agreement.